THE
MISADVENTURES
OF A
SINGLE WOMAN

THE MISADVENTURES OF A SINGLE WOMAN

Sara Jane Coffman

SUNSTONE
PRESS

SANTA FE

Sunstone books may be purchased for educational, business, or sales promotional use.
For information please write: Special Markets Department, Sunstone Press,
P.O. Box 2321, Santa Fe, New Mexico 87504-2321.

Book and Cover design ›Vicki Ahl
Body typeface › Bernhard Modern Std
Printed on acid free paper

Library of Congress Cataloging-in-Publication Data

Coffman, Sara Jane.
  The misadventures of a single woman / by Sara Jane Coffman.
    p. cm.
  ISBN 978-0-86534-828-8 (softcover : alk. paper)
  1. Single women--Humor. 2. Dating (Social customs)--Humor. I. Title.
PN6231.S5485C64 2011
818'.602--dc23
                    2011028479

Published in

WWW.SUNSTONEPRESS.COM
SUNSTONE PRESS / POST OFFICE BOX 2321 / SANTA FE, NM 87504-2321 /USA
(505) 988-4418 / ORDERS ONLY (800) 243-5644 / FAX (505) 988-1025

To the people every Single Woman needs in her life

My contractor, my mechanic, my vet, my attorney, the guy who fixes my
computer, my plumber, my herbalist, my physical therapist,
my massage therapist, my acupuncturist, my personal trainer,
my chiropractor, my hair stylist, my secretary,

And my friends . . . who I hold responsible for my sense of humor

CONTENTS

PREFACE

I toyed with a number of different titles for this book. I thought it might be fun to include some of them here so you can see what you're getting yourself into. Not only will they prepare you for some of the topics in the book, but they'll give you a feel for my writing style, my thinking, and the way I perceive the world.

Alternate Titles:

My Hair's a Mess, My Feet are Always Cold, and I Need a Vacation

I Usually Look Better Than This

The Cat Just Threw Up on the Bed

Is the Boat Rocking, or is it Just Me?

It Seemed Like a Good Idea at the Time

Sally Coffman: Teacher, Writer, Independent Woman

Sally Coffman: Teacher, Writer, Independent Woman, Motorcycle Rider

Sally Coffman: Teacher, Writer, Independent Woman, Motorcycle Rider, Idiot

Once you start writing book titles, it's hard to get them out of your head.

This book reflects my attitude toward life, which is: you can't wait for laughter to come to you. You have to go look for it. For me, the place I find humor most often is in the daily "disasters" I have in my life. Actually, they aren't really disasters. They're minor annoyances, inconveniences, mishaps, and embarrassing moments with an occasional faux pas thrown in.

You don't have to be single—or a woman—to enjoy this book. Regardless of gender or marital status, we all have embarrassing moments and "disasters" in our lives, like getting stuck in an elevator, trying to explain what you want done with your hair at the beauty parlor, and deciding to paint your house with your 16-year-old nephew when neither of you have ever painted a house before.

So, curl up with your blanket and your cats, and enjoy my "misadventures."

They'll probably remind you a lot of your own.

DATING MISADVENTURES

Excuse Me, Your Fly is Open

My friends would describe me as a relatively humble individual, but that hasn't always been the case. For most of my life I've been really full-of-myself. When you're full-of-yourself, you feel it's your duty to go out into the world and try to impress people. Unfortunately, when I try to impress people, I usually end up embarrassing myself. This phenomenon occurs most often when I'm trying to impress a member of the opposite sex.

Take, for example, the Sunday morning I went to the grocery. As I pulled into a parking space, I noticed an attractive guy pulling his car into the space next to mine. He looked over at me and smiled.

Great Sign! I thought. I smiled back.

He got out of his car and started walking toward the store. I followed a few steps behind him. He turned and smiled at me again! I grinned back, thinking "Wow! This is a first! Nobody's ever tried to pick me up at the grocery store before."

He turned and waited at the store entrance. I knew he was going to ask me out. Flashing my most seductive smile, I walked toward him, shoulders back and head held high. I couldn't wait to hear his opening line. Unfortunately, it was: "Did you know you have a flat tire?"

Oh. Sure. I knew that.

Another monumentally embarrassing time occurred when I was going to fly for the first time. I bought beautiful red luggage (so I'd stand out) and spent the morning deciding on just the right outfit (so I'd stand out). My plan was to impress everyone who saw me how sharp I looked and how much I knew about flying. I was going to show people that I was a regular jet-setter, a well-traveled "woman of the world."

At the airport, I waltzed up to the ticket agent, looked him dead in the eye, and declared (so everyone could hear): "I'm here to stand fly-by."

I'd meant to say "fly stand-by," but I'd reversed it.

Instead of being impressed with me, the agent looked at me like I was an idiot. And I felt like one. I was totally humiliated. The moral of the story is: I wasn't a sophisticated jet-setter and shouldn't have tried to act like one.

Sometimes, however, the shoe is on someone else's foot. I once had a date with a rather arrogant psychiatrist (I didn't know he was arrogant until that night) who spent the evening trying to impress me. We were sitting in a theatre waiting for a play to begin when he placed his left ankle on his right knee, leaned back in his seat with his arms on the backs of the chairs on either side of him, surveyed the room, and said: "I think I'm a little overdressed for this crowd, don't you?"

I think he wanted me to comment on his expensive, designer suit. All I could see was that his fly was unzipped. I didn't think he was overdressed at all. I thought he wasn't dressed enough.

I used to think I'd outgrow embarrassing situations, but I know now that's not going to happen. As I've gotten older, they've decreased in number—I'm not trying to show off as much anymore—but they still occur. My philosophy towards them, however, has changed. It's based on a line from the television series *Mash* where Corporal Klinger runs up to Colonel Potter and cries: "But, Colonel, you don't understand! This is the worst day of my life!" Colonel Potter's reply was classic. "Don't be ridiculous. You're going to have a lot worse days than this."

Well, that's become my philosophy. No matter how embarrassing an incident is, I know that someday something worse is going to happen.

Actually, embarrassing situations are good for us. They remind us to lighten up and stop taking ourselves so seriously. The trick is knowing how to react to them. Notice, if you will, the growth in my reaction between my "stand fly-by" incident and my latest embarrassing moment:

I was walking down the street a few days ago when a young man came up to me and said: "Excuse me, ma'am. Did you know you have a pair of pantyhose coming out of your dress?" Then he disappeared.

I looked around for the camera from *America's Funniest Home Videos*. I didn't see it. Then I looked down. My pantyhose were on my legs—right where they should be. What was he talking about? I twisted to the right and saw nothing out of the ordinary. I turned to the left and saw nothing out of the ordinary. Then I gave it one last shot—I twisted completely around and saw that, indeed, there was a pair of pantyhose stuck in my belt—the legs flapping in the breeze.

Was I mortified? Hell, no.

I did what anyone else would do. I pulled the pantyhose out of my belt, stuffed them under my arm, and continued on.

Computer Dating

I was one of the first people to ever try computer dating. Back in the old days there were occasionally ads in the newspaper that gave you an address where you could send away for an application form. Which you filled out by hand. According to the dating service I tried, I would be sent the first names and phone numbers of six "matches." If the computer couldn't find at least three good prospects for me, my money would be refunded.

Feeling reckless, I wet the tip of my pencil in my mouth and began filling out the form. Easy to describe myself—5'1" tall, 105 pounds, curly brown hair. But then I was supposed to describe the kind of guy I was looking for. How tall should he be? Could he be mustached? Sideburned? Bearded? Bald?

I decided for the questions on height to put "no more than twelve inches shorter than me" and "no more than twenty-four inches taller." Regarding facial hair, I said that all types, lengths, and absences were acceptable.

The second section of the questionnaire dealt with attitudes and values. Keeping to my strategy of being open-minded, I responded in favor of everything. On the hobbies and sports section, I checked that I enjoyed everything from hang gliding to deer hunting. Then I mailed it in.

I was watching TV one night a few weeks later, when the phone rang.

"Hello?"

"Sara?"

"This is Sara."

Pause. Heavy breathing.

"This is Fred," a voice said. Who was Fred?

"I'm one of your computer dates." More heavy breathing.

I thought back. Was there a space on the application form "must be able to talk on the phone?" I couldn't remember one.

"Well, I haven't received my computer date list yet," I said cheerfully. "When did you get yours?"

Pause.

"An hour ago." An hour ago?

"Well," I said, trying to move the conversation along. "Would you like to get together for lunch?"

More heavy breathing.

"All right."

As I hung up, I tried to convince myself that Fred would be better in person than he was on the phone. He was probably just shy.

We met at a cafeteria the next day for lunch. Fred looked like a toothpick with a goatee. After we selected our food and approached the cashier, Fred turned to me and said, "I suppose you're going to insist on paying for your own lunch." I assured him that I would.

Contrary to his behavior on the phone, Fred never stopped

talking. He bragged that his family was wealthy, that he was getting his Ph.D. in industrial engineering, and that he had a slew of close friends. My opinion of him was different. I thought he was one of the most obnoxious people I'd ever met.

Finally, lunch ended and I got up to leave. It was then that Fred informed me he'd lost his list of computer dates. I said I was sure the company would send him another copy.

"Oh," he said, looking into my eyes. "I don't need it . . . now."

"Oh, yes," I thought. "Yes you do."

My list of computer dates was waiting for me when I arrived home. Lo and behold, Fred's name was at the top of the list. He looked great—on paper. According to the computer, Fred and I were 91% compatible in background and appearances, 76% compatible in attitudes and values, and 95% compatible in shared interests. If this was my "best" match, I was in trouble.

That evening I received my second computer-date phone call. Ted. At least he waited a day. That was a good sign. He asked me out for coffee. Able to talk on the phone. Another good sign.

I arrived at the coffee shop with a copy of *Glamour* under my arm. Ted was in a booth reading the latest issue of the *Journal of Nematology.* I was wearing heels, white slacks, and a suede jacket with a fur collar. Ted was wearing hiking boots, fatigues, and a brown flannel shirt. That explained why we rated 28% on background and appearances.

Ted wasn't particularly handsome, but he was a great conversationalist. As we talked, he mentioned that he lived in a log cabin in the woods. How did he heat it? He had a wood-burning stove. What did he do at night? He put a stack of logs on the fire before going to bed which lasted until five a.m. when he got up.

Now, this is the Midwest. It gets cold here in the wintertime. Knowing my great fondness of heat, I made a mental note not to become romantically involved with Ted until spring.

Things appeared to be looking up with Ralph, my third computer date. Not only did he sound good on the phone, but the computer rated us as highly compatible. Based on my experience so far, however, I decided to invite my best friend Diane to join us for lunch.

Recently divorced and new to town, Diane was interested in meeting men, too. She and I made an agreement that if I liked Ralph, I'd have first dibs on him. But if I didn't want him (and she did), I'd sell him to her.

As we ordered, I tried to figure out how Ralph and I scored at the 93rd percentile on appearances. He was 6'4" and had a receding hairline. We also differed in that I'd been on a date before—Ralph hadn't. In fact, that was the first thing he told us—that he'd never been on a date before. But now that he was 26, his mother had decided he should find a nice girl and settle down. His mother was looking in Chicago; Ralph was to look here in Lafayette.

Diane kicked me under the table.

How was I to know he'd never been on a date before?

While eating our chili, Ralph asked us what people talked about on dates, how soon after they met he could ask a girl to marry him, how large his wedding should be, and how many children we thought he should have.

Diane kicked me again.

I suddenly remembered she'd been promising to show me the

new wallpaper in her office. We agreed that now would be a good time. We left Ralph sitting at the restaurant crumbling crackers into his chili and trying to decide how many children to have.

I went home and crossed Ralph off my list.

Bernie was computer date number four. Bernie whispered. To try to hear him I had to keep moving my chair closer and closer to his until I was practically in his lap. I also tried lip reading. I still couldn't hear him. How was I going to get to know him if I couldn't hear him?

I went home and crossed Bernie off my list.

Maybe this would work if I tried being the aggressor. I decided to call the next name on my list—Bruce.

As I dialed his number, I suddenly remembered that a psychic once told me I was going to marry a man named Bruce. To think, I'd been sitting here all this time with the name of my future husband in front of me!

The phone rang. Bruce answered. I introduced myself. "I don't believe this!" he cried. "I was sitting here thinking about calling you!"

He suggested dinner at a local Chinese restaurant—my favorite restaurant!

I was drinking hot tea when Bruce came in and sat down. He looked at me and said: "I can't believe you called me."

I smiled.

"I mean, I can't believe *you* called *me*. You must have dozens of men calling you."

We ordered. Bruce got the $5.95 buffet and barely touched it. I got a double order of beef and peapods and ate the whole thing.

All through dinner Bruce kept shaking his head and repeating,

"I can't believe you called me." Then he'd chuckle. "That's really something—to think you called me." That's all the farther the conversation got. I left Bruce (with the bill) sitting at the Chinese restaurant, went home, and crossed Bruce off my list. Maybe I just wasn't cut out to be a computer date.

But there was one last name on my list. There was still a chance that he was "the one." With great determination, I went to the phone and dialed Moose's number.

I identified myself and told him he was one of my computer dates.

Moose cried, "Hey, baby, you lucked out!"

Uh, Okay. For a moment I considered hanging up. Did I really want to date a guy named "Moose"? But I plunged ahead and invited him to lunch. Knowing that I didn't want to do Moose alone, I called Diane and asked her to join us.

I arrived at the restaurant early and hid behind the coat rack so I could see Moose before he saw me. Moose arrived promptly at noon. At least, I figured that was Moose. An exact duplicate of John Belushi, he was eyeing all the women and grinning. He had a beard and greasy hair. His belly hung down over the front of his pants. He was wearing an army jacket and a dirty yellow T-shirt with the words "Hug me, Baby" across the front. There was a knife sticking out of his boots. He was the most unsavory-looking person I'd ever seen. And he was definitely looking for someone.

I waited a few more minutes to see if someone else might show up. Then I looked at Moose again to see if there was any chance he could be my Prince Charming. No way.

Knowing I couldn't go through with lunch, I sneaked out the

door to head Diane off. I met her hurrying to the rendezvous and explained the situation. Diane, who's never done an immoral thing in her life, told me I could not stand this guy up. I'd made a date with him and I had to follow through. So she marched me back to the restaurant. She walked right up to Moose, said "Hello," then walked past him and took a seat at one of the tables. I scurried after her.

"There is no way we're having lunch with that guy," she said.

Obviously, computer dating is not my thing. I guess I'm the kind of girl who wants to meet a stranger across a crowded room, not have a computer pick him out for me.

It has occurred to me, however, that maybe the trick is in how you fill out the application form.

Maybe things would be different if I tried internet dating.

Where's my laptop?

Opposites Attract

The first time you go out with someone, you look for things you have in common. If you find some, you go out again. If you don't find any, you don't. Right?

Not in my case. In my case I once dated . . . drum roll . . . my complete opposite.

I met Captain Turner in a class I was taking at the local university. He wasn't wearing a uniform, so at first, I didn't know he was in the Army. But as I was looking around the room and checking everyone out the first day, I could tell there was something different about him. Something that set him apart.

Then it hit me. It was his hair. He didn't have any. I mean, he had some, but it was so short you could barely see it. I figured he'd been ill and his hair was just beginning to grow back.

Class began with the professor asking us to introduce ourselves. He announced we could get extra points in the class if we were from his home state (Ohio) or had attended his alma mater (Indiana University). The women in the class could get even more points if they went to the Women's Clinic in town, since that's where the professor's wife worked.

Despite the groundwork, the introductions were pretty boring. Then it was Captain Turner's turn. He stated he was born in Cincinnati, had once visited I.U., and would be happy to start going to the Women's Clinic if that would improve his grade.

I gave him a point for wit.

When class was over, Captain Turner and I left the room at the same time. I was headed back to my office. I asked where he was going.

"To get my hair cut," he said. "I've been meaning to get it cut all week, but this is the first chance I've had."

He was kidding, right?

The next thing I discovered about Turner—besides his sense of humor and his absence of hair—was his complete naiveté about civilian academic life. For example, he was totally unskilled in the art of passing notes. I learned this when I sent him a note congratulating him on a presentation he'd just made.

I wrote the note, inserted it in a textbook, and passed the book to the back of the room. When he got it, he looked at it, puzzled.

"This isn't mine," he mouthed politely when the professor turned to write on the board. What a nerd. Of course it wasn't his.

I motioned for him to pass the book back. I opened it, held the note up for him to see, reinserted it into the book, and passed the book back. When he got it, he still just sat there and smiled.

Patiently, I motioned for him to pass the book back again and went through my pantomime a second time. By now, everyone in the class, including the professor, was waiting for him to open the book and read the note.

Who doesn't know how to pass notes in class?

The more Turner and I talked, the more obvious it became that we had opposite habits, values, and world-views. Take, for example, Turner's approach to class (which was logical and organized). In good military tradition, he read the assignment prior to class, arrived to class on time, and took notes in an official-looking notebook.

I, on the other hand, approached class creatively. Disdainful of routine, I read the assignment if I felt like it, arrived to class at different times, and took notes on whatever I happened to have with me. A check from my checkbook. A borrowed sheet of paper. A styrofoam cup. The back of my hand. But our approaches to education were just the tip of the iceberg.

Turner's whole world was as organized as his notes. I can't stand organization; I like spontaneity. Take, for example, my silverware drawer. I have 56 pieces of silverware (my mother thought I needed that much) in a pile in a drawer. Whenever I need a utensil, I reach in and pull out the piece that's on top. Whatever it happens to be, that's what I use. (I can scramble eggs with knives, forks, and spoons.)

I was happy with this system. It was flexible. I never had to make any decisions. But one evening I invited Turner over for dinner. As he was helping me dry the dishes, he opened my silverware drawer to put something away. I saw him open his mouth to say something, but nothing came out. He simply laid the silverware carefully on top of the pile. The next time he came to dinner, however, he brought me a bright red silverware divider and spent the evening sorting my silverware into the appropriate slots.

I should be grateful, but I'm not. Instead of just opening the drawer and throwing the silverware in like I used to, now I have to stand and carefully sort each piece into its proper spot. Not only is it time-consuming and uncreative, I don't think the silverware is as happy as it used to be.

I had no idea to what extent Turner believed in organization until he invited me to dinner at his apartment. As I was drying his silverware, he opened the drawer, pointed to an empty spot, and said: "That's where the potato peeler goes."

Holy cow! Nobody knows where their potato peeler goes. My mother doesn't even know where her potato peeler goes. (FYI: a potato peeler goes between your pizza cutter and your corn-on-the-cob holders.) After seeing how organized his kitchen was, I got curious about his closets. I organize my closets the same way I organize my silverware. I could never decide whether to arrange my clothes by color, size, length, age, price, or category, so I've never hung them in any order.

When I asked to see one of his closets, it was exactly what I'd expected. The shirts were all on the right, the pants were all on the left, and the hangers—all facing the same direction—were exactly the same distance apart.

Besides differing on organization, Turner and I also differed on how to have fun, and how to spend money. To me, a great evening was getting dressed up and eating at an expensive restaurant. To Turner, a great evening was going to the gym and running five miles. The times he didn't invite me out to run, he invited me to swim, play racquetball, or lift weights.

Turner also had his own ideas of what to buy a woman as a gift. In the months we knew each other, he gave me a pair of running shoes, a racquetball racquet, and a six-month membership to the local racquetball club. I could never tell if he liked me or just thought

I was out of shape. My mother had warned me about men bearing perfume and flowers, but never about one bearing silverware dividers and running shoes.

I guess I never really knew where I stood with Turner, which was all right because just about the time that I realized we were probably too different to ever have a relationship, he finished the program he was taking and returned to active duty.

We did have an effect on each other, though.

I'm getting used to my silverware divider.

And the last time I heard from Turner, he admitted he's been opening his silverware drawer and just throwing his potato peeler in.

Canoe Pulling

People who live where they have to stay cooped up all winter tend to spend a lot of time fantasizing about warm weather, being outside in the sunshine with their friends, and having fun. Tom, the pilot I've been dating, belongs to a group of aviators who spent all last winter fantasizing about going canoeing. In mid-January, on the coldest day of the year, they decided to go on a six-hour canoe trip the first nice Saturday in summer.

For months, they planned the trip in minute detail, as carefully as if they were planning a cross-country flight. The club members were eager. Young. Strong. Athletic. When summer arrived, they checked the weather reports (as only pilots can do) and found a day that was going to be warm and sunny with just a hint of cool breeze. Exactly the kind of day they'd dreamed about all winter.

The only thing they hadn't planned on was the drought.

The thing is, there's a direct relationship between a drought and the amount of water in a creek. And it's hard to go canoeing when there's no water in the creek. What you do is end up engaging in an activity we now fondly refer to as "canoe pulling."

Not just anyone can go canoe pulling. Real canoeists, for

example, check the water depth before they go on a trip. Canoe pulling is performed only by people who've been cooped up all winter and who don't think about things like water depth. Well, eventually they do—when the canoes they're launching scrape the bottom. (Note: You can always tell the amount of water in the creek by the speed with which the canoe rental employees jump into their trucks and take off from the launch site.)

In case you've never gone canoe pulling and would like to know what it's like, here are some statistics from our trip that will shed some light. Picture this: I was manning the front of the canoe; Tom was manning the rear.

Total number of miles we planned to canoe: six

Number of miles the water was deep enough so we could use our paddles: one

Number of times I yelled: "Rock!": 682

Number of times we drove up onto and got stuck on rocks: 682

Number of times Tom said "Shit": 682

Number of times Tom had to get out of the canoe, walk to the front, and pull the canoe off the rock: 682

Number of times Tom disengaged the canoe and its passenger from the rock gently: the first five

The moral of the story is this: if you're thinking about going canoeing, check to make sure there's enough water in the creek.

Checking water depth was just one thing I learned from our trip. I also learned that men and women should never canoe together. The canoes that were manned by males and females spent as much time turned sideways as they did facing forward. That's because, genetically, men and women have different approaches to canoeing.

For example, Tom's approach to getting the canoe through a tight spot was to use force and speed. My approach was to remain calm and let the canoe ease through the opening on its own. So at critical moments, Tom would paddle his end of the canoe like crazy, while I put the brakes on at my end. Either of our approaches would have worked with collaboration. What we did was cancel each other out.

Another reason men and women shouldn't canoe together is because canoeing requires communication. Even simple words, like "left" and "right" mean different things in a canoe depending on your sex. It wasn't until the trip was over that I realized every time I'd yelled: "Right!" Tom had paddled on the right. That, of course, made the canoe go left. What I'd meant was that I wanted him to paddle on the left so the canoe would go right. This could explain why we hit so many rocks.

But we weren't the only ones. All the couples seemed to be fighting. Trust me. You will not feel more loving towards your partner after a canoe trip. Canoeing was invented for the sole purpose of testing relationships, not bringing people closer together.

If you're planning a canoe trip, I think it might help if you could agree on some things prior to launch. (Like what is meant by "left" and "right.") You should also agree on what you'll each do in the event you capsize. The agreement I had with Tom was that he would rescue me before he rescued the cooler. To reinforce the likelihood of his doing so, I wore his favorite baseball hat. When he tried desperately to talk me out of wearing it before we left, I knew I'd be safe.

Part of the fun of canoeing (or canoe pulling) is being hot, sweaty, miserable, and uncomfortable from the time you leave your car until the time you return to it. The misery begins with the bus ride from the canoe rental place to the launch site. Our bus had just one gear, no brakes, no windshield wipers, no door, and no shock absorbers. The windows wouldn't open, and the driver never turned the engine off for fear it wouldn't restart. The bus had been running nonstop since 1964.

What the bus trip does is make you look forward to getting your canoe in the water (even though you know you won't see any shade for six hours.) Be sure to take sunscreen. And plenty of stuff to drink. Wear a hat. Take food. If done correctly, there's little opportunity to stretch your legs in a canoe, so don't plan any activities that require standing up straight for the next few days.

Take insect repellent. Mosquitoes like to go canoeing, too. Wear your oldest pair of shoes, and plan to throw them away after the trip. Creek water is notoriously smelly, and even though Tom never made me get out and push, he kept bringing water into the canoe with him when he got back in. He weighs twice what I do, so the water in the bottom of the canoe remained in the back with him. Until he got out. Then it rushed to the front, ruining my shoes. After the trip, we both had to throw our shoes away.

Watch out for tree branches hanging over the water. Young snakes see canoes as a convenient way to visit their relatives downstream. And lastly, if you're busy paddling in the front of the canoe and your partner yells "Duck!"—do it. You can always ask questions later.

Canoeing is a great sport. Especially for people who want to relax and enjoy the outdoors. One couple had the right idea. They put a huge cooler of beer in the middle of their canoe, got comfortable, and just drifted.

They were the first ones back to the canoe rental place.

How Not to Meet Men

Sometimes I have a hard time meeting men. There aren't a lot of men where I work, and I don't go to singles bars. So, what's a girl to do?

Well, according to an article I read in a singles' magazine, if I wanted to meet men, I'd have to go where the men were. I wasn't going to meet a man in my pilates class or at my community theatre's production of *My Fair Lady*. I needed to hang out at small airports, gyms, and auto body shops. A gym seemed the lesser of those evils, so I bought a pair of running shoes and joined the local health club.

The article was right: The track at the health club was filled with lots of delicious-looking, lean, male bodies. I didn't want to look like the "newbie at the gym," so I positioned myself near a group of runners and tried to copy what they were doing. They had their legs crossed and were bending over, touching their toes. I bent over to touch my toes. Not even close. So I squatted down and pretended to tie my shoelaces so I could eavesdrop.

The main topic of conversation seemed to be an upcoming race called the Hog Jog. It seemed like everyone was going to run in the race. The men didn't ask each other: "Are you going to run the Hog Jog?" It was always: "Are you running the 5K or the 10K?" Once distance had been determined, there was the issue of speed. It seemed appropriate to ask if the runner was thinking about going for a P.R. (personal record) or if he thought his injuries (bad knee, pulled muscle, torn ligament) were going to hold him back.

I looked around and saw a female runner who was cooling down from her run. I started walking alongside her.

"I'm new here. Know anything about the Hog Jog?"

"Oh," she said, wiping her face. "That's where Karen met her husband."

Do tell.

"Karen moved here from out East. She met Jon when they were running together during the race, and a month later they were married."

Suddenly, I was highly motivated to run in the Hog Jog.

According to the application form, the Hog Jog heralds the start of the Carroll County Pork Festival. Held in Flora, Indiana (population 2,000), it boasts that it's the only race where you'll see more pigs along the route than you will people. There was more: All those showing up for the race would receive a free "Hog Jog" T-shirt. Those who finished the race would also receive a free pork burger. How could I pass up a deal like that?

I signed up for the 5K run and practiced jogging (on and off) for the next few weeks. Truth be told, I wasn't that interested in the race. I was going to meet men.

I arrived in Flora the day of the race. The registration table was in the park in the center of town. There were colorful balloons tied to the trees, tents with picnic tables set up for refreshments, and the smell of pork sausage in the air. And there were men! Lots and lots of good-looking men.

They were drinking from water bottles, chatting with each other, and bending over to touch their toes. I had on a new T-shirt and a new pair of shorts and I knew I looked good. I noticed, however, that the men seemed more interested in the race than they were in me. That was okay. I'd just wait and strike up a conversation with someone along the route while we were running. Like Karen did.

The officials called for the start of the longer race, the 10K, and all of the gorgeous, lean bodies lined up in the road. Seconds later, they were gone, leaving me standing in the dust with the women, children, and men over 75 who were going to run in the 5K race. It hadn't occurred to me that the men I was interested in would be running the longer race. There was no way I could run 10 kilometers. As I stood there covered in dust, I decided to go ahead and run the shorter race, and then get in shape next year for the 10K.

Now that the men were gone, I started to notice the heat and humidity. It was June. In Indiana. It occurred to me that I could die, just standing in the heat, let alone running in it. To distract myself, I glanced around at my competition. Some runners were jogging in place, some were leaning forward in a runner's crouch, and some were waving to their loved ones on the sidelines. I moved away from a croucher, closer to a waver.

The gun went off! The joggers, crouchers, and wavers all ran off, leaving me trailing the pack. No sweat, I told myself. I'll pass them along the way.

The first leg of the run was alongside a cornfield. We were running into a strong wind. I discovered I'd pinned my race number too high on my chest and was temporarily blinded when the wind blew the number up into my face. I held the number down with my left hand and continued on. The wind then entered the space between my baseball hat and my head, and I was in serious danger of losing my hat. That couldn't happen because I hadn't done my hair. My hat was an integral part of my outfit.

I reached up with my right hand and held onto my hat. It didn't take long to realize I wasn't going to make very good time running with one hand on my chest and the other hand on my head. I took my hat off, crumpled it in my hand, and moved my number lower on my shirt.

As I made the first turn, I found I had two additional problems. I'd forgotten to leave my keys in my car so my keys were bouncing around in my pocket. The change I'd received after paying my entry fee was trying to escape from my other pocket. I stuffed the money back in.

My problems thus solved, I could now concentrate on the race. This was unfortunate, because the only thing there was to think about was the heat. And the fact that we weren't halfway through yet. And the fact that I hadn't passed anyone yet. And the fact that the EMT vehicle and the people walking the race were just a few steps behind me.

We turned, left the cornfield-lined road, and passed through a residential area. The townspeople were standing on their porches— mute—watching us go by. Occasionally, I'd see a smile or hear a word of encouragement, but for the most part, the runners and the townspeople just stared at each other.

The heat was unbearable. My face was burning up. I couldn't

get my breath. I decided to stop and walk for a minute. As I passed a group of farmers standing in the doorway of the bank, I heard one of them say: "Well, that's the end of the first group. These are just the walkers." I held my head up and thought: "Listen, buddy, I don't see you out here."

Their scoffing gave me my motivation to finish the face. My goal of passing anyone—people in wheelchairs, people on crutches, people with grey hair, women running with strollers, children in wheelchairs, children on crutches, children with grey hair—was long gone.

Fortunately, the last leg of the run was downhill and shady. No, wait. It was uphill. It couldn't be uphill. Why would they make it uphill? It was uphill! At least the noise level had picked up—people were actually cheering on the sidelines. I started singing the theme from Rocky in my head. There it was! The finish line! I'd made it to the finish line!

I collapsed on all fours under the nearest tree. A young boy came over to ask if I was all right.

"Water," I wheezed. He returned a few seconds later carrying not one, but two cups.

After I sat there for awhile, I started to recover. I uncrumpled my hat and put it back on so I'd be ready to strike up a conversation with the 10K runners when they finished.

But as they crossed the finish line, they were the sorriest-looking group of people I'd ever seen. They looked like a bunch of drowned rats. I remember thinking: "I just ran five kilometers for this?" And they didn't hang around. When they were finished with the race, they picked up their T-shirts and pork burgers and headed to their cars.

So, not only had I NOT met a man, I was hot, my muscles were sore, and my heart was beating like someone in the last stages of congestive heart failure. I picked up my T-shirt and my free pork burger and limped to my car.

Surely there had to be a better way to meet men.

Maybe I should try flying lessons.

Flannel Shirts

Shirt color was always high on my list of criteria when it came to dating. I dated men in white shirts, not blue. You would never have found me out with any of the following:

The really rough ice road truckers they show on the History channel who drive huge trucks over frozen lakes.

Men who wear bowling shirts (when they're not in a bowling alley).

"Bleacher bums" at ballgames who suck beer out of straws connected to their hats.

Suspicious-looking men wearing trench coats.

Shirtless guys in the infield at the Indianapolis 500 who yell "Show me your tits."

Guys who wear white T-shirts (with holes in the armpits) for their high school pictures.

Guys who don't have high school pictures.

I was such a snob, in fact, I freaked out when I read that Katherine Hepburn said she enjoyed making *Rooster Cogburn* with John Wayne. A cowboy? How could someone as classy, sophisticated, and elegant as Katherine Hepburn have agreed to make a movie about a cowboy?

When I read in her autobiography that what she liked most about making the movie was leaning up against John Wayne when they were on his horse, and that she did it "as often as possible," I had to stop reading.

How could anyone feel that way about a cowboy?

Then I had a chance encounter with a cop, who stepped into my world of academia. He was well-read, especially in the field of American history. He loved talking about the Civil War, airplanes, and WWII. He could build things and fix things. He loved to travel. He loved the outdoors. He was sensitive to women's issues. He listened. He had a good relationship with his mother. He was down-to-earth, practical, and real. Everything I wanted in a man, except that he wore a blue shirt.

Actually, when he was off-duty, he wore flannel shirts. That's what got me hooked. One evening when we were watching TV, I leaned up against his chest to see what it would feel like. It was the first time I'd ever leaned up against a flannel shirt.

It was warm.

And fuzzy.

And cozy.

It felt good. Different from a white shirt. You can't cuddle with a white shirt. You either slide off, or you have to worry about leaving your makeup on them. But flannel shirts? Damned sexy.

When I finally got up the courage to tell one of my equally elitist friends that I was dating a cop, she confessed she was dating a farmer.

"You're kidding! Does he wear flannel shirts?" I asked, remembering all of our late-night conversations about our standards for dating men.

"Does he ever," she sighed dreamily. "I fell in love with him because of his shirts."

So they got to her, too.

Thanks to my blue-shirted cop, I've been doing all sorts of things I never dreamed of doing, like camping in the rain, hiking in the fog, riding a motorcycle on curvy back roads, seeing where Custer had his last stand, and shooting a pistol on a firing range. Plus I've learned a bunch of neat stuff, like:

Put Kleenex in your pocket before taking a walk in the woods.

Riding on the back of a motorcycle is really cool.

Riding on the back of a motorcycle in the rain is even cooler. (Even though you have to cover up in amazingly unfashionable, bright yellow rain gear.)

Motorcyclists aren't as scary as they look. In fact, they're pretty neat people. If I ever get in a fix, I'll go to a motorcycle rider for help.

Keep a first aid kit, and survival gear, in your trunk.

Camouflage jackets (admittedly unfashionable) are warm.

Russian army fur hats with ear flaps (even more unfashionable) are even warmer.

Dating a cop expanded my world by leaps and bounds. When I finally came down from my ivory tower, I discovered I'd dismissed a lot of neat people and missed out on a lot of wonderful things in my life, like the fact that rough hands can be gentle.

So—if you've been judging men on the basis of how expensive their ties are, here's some advice. The guy you're looking for may not even wear a tie. He may be dressed in a camouflage jacket and army boots.

Katherine Hepburn knew what she was doing the whole time.

Trying to Change a Man

$\mathcal{Y}$es, I watch Oprah. Yes, I've seen the shows where women confess they've tried to change the men in their lives. Yes, I've heard Oprah ask:

"Didn't you know that he drank (played around, wore women's clothing) before you got married?"

Guest (sobbing): "But I thought he'd change!"

Give me a break! We all know you should love people for who they are, not who you can make them into. Which brings me to my bicycle story. I need to explain that this is an entirely different scenario. I was not trying to change my significant other. I was only trying to help him.

When J.R.'s job became more stressful, he coped by sitting at his computer in the evenings and playing computer games. It occurred to me that a better way for him to relieve his stress would be to get more exercise. He wasn't the kind of guy who'd go to a health club, but he did own a 10-speed bike. I figured if I bought a bike, I could ask him to go riding with me under the guise of getting me in shape. It was a devious (but foolproof) plan.

That weekend, I found a bike at a garage sale and asked J.R.

to check it out for me. After fiddling with it for a few minutes, he proclaimed it seaworthy. It was practically brand new. The owner explained she'd bought it several years ago and just never had time to ride it. We offered her $50.00 which she readily accepted. Actually, she seemed rather glad to be getting rid of it. As we drove off with the bike in the back of the truck, I saw her grinning and waving.

Now, the last time I was on a bike you peddled the pedals backwards to stop. This bike had hand brakes, 10 gears, and thin little tires. The tires intrigued me. In the middle of each tire was an almost imperceptible little strip of rubber. I asked J.R. what it was for.

"It's what you ride on," he said.

Really? Interesting.

That evening he took me to the cemetery so I could practice. I held onto the handlebars of the bike and ran alongside until I got the courage to hop up. But getting up was nothing compared to staying up. If I could do this, I could join a circus. It occurred to me that this could be dangerous. Then I remembered my goal—to get J.R. in shape.

The next thing I needed to do was master the hand brakes. It felt strange knowing that my hands were controlling the brakes instead of my feet. As I was descending my first hill, building up speed, I heard J.R. call "Use your hand brakes!" He had to yell because he was sitting on the tailgate of his truck with his legs stretched out in front of him, drinking a Big Gulp.

After circling the cemetery a few times, I decided it was time to get J.R. out there. He agreed to take me for a ride the following morning.

Sunday morning arrived, bright and shiny—a beautiful day for a bike ride.

"Why don't we have breakfast first," he suggested. That sounded good, so we went to breakfast. After breakfast, I announced I was ready to go.

"You really should have a helmet," J.R. offered. So we went to Wal-Mart and bought a helmet. While we were there, he decided he could use a new pair of shorts. So he bought a pair of shorts. On our way out, he mentioned I should get a lock for my bike. So we backtracked to sporting goods and bought a lock. By the time we got home, it was almost noon.

I donned my new helmet, hooked my new lock onto the handlebars of my bike, and announced that I was ready to go. J.R. went to the storage shed to get his bike. In the far corner of the shed, directly above his bike, was a huge wasp's nest. J.R. stood and watched the wasps.

"I think if we wait a few days, they'll move on," he said.

"We're going for a ride today," I said.

"I'll bet there's a way to move the nest," my lover-of-insects-and-animals explained. "Let me see what I can find." He returned to his computer and began reading up on moving wasp's nests. After sulking for about an hour, I went over, shut his computer off, and ordered him to go get his bike. Wasps or no wasps. I must have been a worse threat than the wasps, because he went to the shed and retrieved his bicycle. The wasps couldn't have cared less.

Just as we mounted up, there was a loud rumble in the sky and it began to rain. It rained all day. So ended our first day of bike riding. J.R. promised to take me for a ride after work the next day.

Monday evening. J.R. arrived home and saw me standing in his driveway next to my bike.

"Why don't we have dinner before we ride?" he said.

"Mount up," I said, smacking him in the stomach with his helmet. We started out.

Sullivan, Indiana is a perfect town for a bike ride. There was a little gas station where we got air in our tires. The tree-lined streets had couples rocking on their porches and kids playing basketball in their driveways. The air was cool and fresh as it blew past my face. As we passed the house where I bought my bike, the lady came out on her porch and waved. Was she still grinning? Probably just my imagination.

As we rode, I began to notice things. Like it took every bit of energy for me to stay balanced up on my teeny, tiny strip of rubber. The slightest breeze propelled me from the middle of the street up into people's front lawns. Once, I scratched an itch and ended up in a lady's flower bed.

J.R., on the other hand, was riding with his hands clasped behind his head and flattening empty pop cans as he rode down the street. I suddenly became aware of the fact that HIS tires were thick and knurly, like snow tires. Anybody could ride on tires like that!

"Why didn't you tell me my bike had teeny little tires when I bought it?" I demanded.

"You didn't ask."

I also noticed that he was riding circles around me (literally), effortlessly, while I was pedaling my legs off.

"Why is that? I asked, gasping for air, as we stopped at an intersection.

"You're not switching gears."

Gears?

He tried to explain the gear system to me. It was way over my head. I longed for my high school bike that I could just jump on and ride. I decided to learn about gears some other time. About the time that my brain gave out, my body gave out as well. I cried "Uncle" and we headed home. I was exhausted; J.R. hadn't broken a sweat or been affected by the ride in the least.

The next day, when the alarm went off, J.R. hopped out of bed as usual. I couldn't move. During the night, someone had put screws in my joints and tightened them as tightly as they could. I creaked as I got out of bed. I could hardly walk. I had to raise my arms in tiny increments to get dressed.

"Honey," I said, "when we were riding last night, why didn't you mention that I might not want to do too much my first time out?"

Bending over easily to tie his shoelaces, he said cheerfully: "Because you'd already accused me of not wanting to go for a ride."

I concede. J.R.is in much better shape than I am.

I'm going to put my bike out on the curb and hope someone takes it.

And I'm going to start playing computer games in the evenings, too.

PROBLEMS WITH FAMILY AND FRIENDS

Becoming a Father

I was sitting in my apartment grading papers one evening when there was a knock on my door. It was my next door neighbor, Cassey, with some exciting news. She was pregnant.

For as long as I'd known Cassey, I'd known she'd wanted to have a baby. I also knew the baby's father was out of the picture and that her family lived out of town. She wasn't going to have much of a support system. So I said: "Cassey, if there's anything I can do to help. . ." You know how you always say that, but you never really mean it?

Well, Cassey took me up on it. She wanted to attend childbirth classes. Would I go with her?

Now, I knew nothing about "birthin' babies." But as a teacher, I'm a great believer in learning new things. It might be interesting. It would probably be sort of like taking bowling lessons. So I agreed to go.

We arrived early to the first class and watched the other couples arrive. Without fail, the wives would enter first and walk up to the instructor's desk to fill out a name tag. The husbands, on the other hand, usually made it no farther than the doorway. The fact that they carried large, fluffy pillows didn't make their entrances any easier.

Even though they tried to act as if it were perfectly natural for them to be carrying large, fluffy pillows, they looked like they'd all been dragged to class and would rather be home watching Monday night football.

The instructor began by asking the husbands when they were expecting their babies. None of them knew. It occurred to me that I had no idea when Cassey's baby was due.

"When is your baby due?" I leaned over and asked.

"February eighteenth."

That was nice. February would be a good month to have a baby. As long as there wasn't a blizzard.

After a short lecture, the instructor asked the women to get down on the floor for exercises, and the men to remain seated. I looked around, trying to decide which group to join. I remained seated.

The instructor explained that our group would be called "coaches," but she soon fell back to referring to the two groups as "the mothers" and "the fathers." It suddenly dawned on me that the instructor thought I was going through the delivery with Cassey. I was going to have to correct her on that one. But by agreeing to attend classes, had I automatically agreed to go through the delivery? And if I didn't, who would?

Maybe this wasn't going to be like taking bowling lessons.

For the next few days, I tried to figure out how I felt about going through the delivery. I decided to try the idea out on an old friend from high school. I called Lora Bell.

"And so I'm going to be a father. I'm going through the delivery with Cassey and everything," I bragged.

Silence on the other end of the line.

"What's wrong?" I asked.

"Don't you remember that health course we took our freshman year? What happened to you during the movie on childbirth?"

Oh, yeah. As soon as the opening title had appeared on the screen, I had to bend over and put my head between my knees. As Lora Bell watched the film, she fanned me with her notebook.

The last thing I wanted to do was disappoint Cassey in the delivery room, so I told her she'd better not count on me for anything except going to classes with her. She said that was all right. That's all she'd ever asked.

My favorite class was when we discussed what the fathers should do to prepare for the trip to the hospital.

"Get gas in the car!" I called out enthusiastically.

"Right!" the instructor said.

"Learn how to get to the hospital without crossing any railroad tracks," offered Cassey. In our town, getting from point A to point B without crossing railroad tracks was a real feat. There were tracks crossing all of the major roads, and invariably, whenever you were in a hurry to get somewhere, you'd get stopped by a train.

Then we discussed food. Although the mothers weren't supposed to eat on their way to the hospital, the instructor said the fathers should eat to keep up their strength. She even suggested stopping and buying a bagful of doughnuts.

Now, if you add those things up—get gas in the car, know how to get to the hospital without crossing railroad tracks, and eat a bagful of doughnuts—it sounded like something I could handle. So, I told Cassey that when the time came, I'd like to drive her to the hospital. I wouldn't stay with her, but I'd see that she got there.

The final session came and we all received certificates for having completed the course. According to mine, I was now a prepared parent.

February arrived. The good news was, the baby came right on schedule. The bad news was, it was in the middle of the biggest blizzard of the decade.

Two a.m. I was sleeping soundly, tucked under a pile of warm blankets, when the phone rang. I answered it and Cassey said: "It's time to go to the hospital."

Now, when I'd offered to take her to the hospital, I'd meant that I'd do it in the daytime—not in the middle of the night. And not in the cold! I hate being cold! I considered asking her to call me back in the morning.

Then it hit me! This was my big moment! This is when I was going to drive Cassey slowly and responsibly to the hospital!

I jumped out of bed, pulled on my clothes, and started loading the car with everything I thought we might need—my Nikon, pop tarts, a frozen coffee cake (I was supposed to eat to keep my strength up), two *Working Mother* magazines, a deck of cards, a flashlight, and an armload of towels in case her water broke in the car.

When I went to get Cassey, the wind almost blew us over. The snow was falling so fast we couldn't see. We had to push our way through some waist-high snow drifts to get to my car. Getting her into the bucket seat of my sports car wasn't easy. We'd practiced getting into the car, but not with her quite that pregnant. I gently pushed her stomach in and got the door closed. The temperature (we found out later) was 15 below zero. The wind chill was 20 below. I couldn't believe we were doing this!

Cassey had a contraction. I tried to chat pleasantly with her as I drove slowly and calmly over the icy road. Cassey had another contraction. I hunched over the wheel, reduced my speed, and increased my determination not to let her interfere with my plans for a slow, calm trip to the hospital. Cassey had another contraction. Then she asked if I'd brought the stop watch.

I'd forgotten the one thing I was supposed to bring.

I dropped Cassey off at the emergency entrance, parked the car in a snow drift, and hurried into the hospital lugging her suitcase and all the paraphernalia I'd brought. As it turned out, her labor was quite far along. I was so fascinated that something exciting was happening that I took my coat off and started visiting with everyone. Cassey didn't want to play cards like I thought she would, but she seemed glad for my company.

When the doctor arrived (by snowmobile), he immediately told Cassey she could push. Suddenly the nurses cried, "We're going to have a baby!" and rushed out of the room. They returned with a gurney to take Cassey to the delivery room. From their speed, it looked like they thought the baby was going to be born in transit.

The nurses told me if I wanted to go into the delivery room with them that I should get a gown at the nurse's station. Did I want to go into the delivery room with them? Wild horses wouldn't have kept me from seeing the final action!

I rushed to the nurse's station and asked for a gown.

"You'll have to get permission from the doctor to enter the delivery room," the head nurse said in her best professional manner. I panicked. Out of the corner of my eye, I could see them wheeling

Cassey into the delivery room. If I didn't hurry, I was going to miss it.

"Oh," I said, pulling myself up to my entire 5'1" height. "I'm the baby's *father*. The doctor is expecting me."

Eyeing me suspiciously, she handed me a gown. I dashed into the nearest bathroom and pulled it on over my head. Seconds later, I was standing in the delivery room.

Now, maybe my memory is faulty, or maybe I was dreaming at the time, but what I recall is that they tilted the bed Cassey was on, and the baby slid right out.

The doctor laid him on Cassey's stomach and the nurses covered him with warm blankets. I lifted them a bit so Cassey and I could peek in. He made gurgling noises and seemed content to just lie there and rest. Cassey and I both grinned.

The experience was nothing like taking bowling lessons, but it was the most exciting night in my life. So, the next time you have a chance to say: "If there's anything I can do to help," I hope you say it.

You never know what might happen.

You, too, might have the chance to become a father.

Surviving My Parents' Visits

It's always traumatic when my parents come to visit. Why is it I can be living on my own, self-sufficient and self-reliant, yet visits from my parents make me stutter, mutter, and want to bang my head against the wall?

The problem with my parents is, when I'm living under their roof, I'm expected to obey their rules. And when they're living under my roof . . . I'm expected to obey their rules.

Here's a typical visit from my parents. See if any of the games we play sound familiar.

Game #1: Arriving a day early.

My parents live in Philadelphia. When they come to visit me in Indiana they pack their car with so many suitcases, boxes of food, golf clubs, and emergency equipment that the stuff explodes when they open the car doors. The problem, however, is not what they bring, it's their time of arrival. They always arrive a day early. Since I put off getting groceries and cleaning the house until the last minute, they always arrive to a dirty, foodless house.

I know. If I know this is going to happen, why don't I prepare even earlier for their visits? I did. The last time they visited, I was ready a day early.

They arrived two days in advance.

Game #2: Fleas. Fleas. Who's got the fleas?

My parents have a key to my house so naturally they're standing in the doorway when I get home from work. Before greeting me or finding out how I am, their first comment is: "You've got fleas." Now, my cats have never had fleas. But whenever my parents come to visit, they insist they've found fleas and that we have to bomb the house. So I take Heathcliff and Suey to a friend's house while my parents go to the hardware store and buy the flea bombs. My dad sets the bombs off—one on each floor—while my mom and I run outside and jump in the car.

We eat, do some shopping, then arrive home well before we're supposed to. If the directions on the bomb say "leave the house for four hours," we're back in two. The temperature outside could be 25 degrees, but that doesn't stop my parents. They just open the windows. They're immune to the smell. It makes the cats and me cough and wheeze. We all go to bed that first night exhausted, but at least my parents are convinced there are no more fleas.

If you ask me, I think it's my parents who have fleas.

Game #3: Where are we going to sleep?

While we're working on the problem with the fleas, we're

simultaneously trying to work out the sleeping arrangements. This discussion—repeated verbatim every time they come to visit—rivals the Abbott and Costello classic: "Who's on first?" We play "Where should we sleep?"

The choices are: my large bedroom (upstairs) and a teeny tiny guest room (downstairs). The guest bedroom is so small that the bed takes up the entire room. It's like being on a sleeper coach on a train—you have to go into the bathroom to change into your pajamas. You then open the bathroom door and lay right down on the bed. So I try to get them to stay upstairs in my room.

"Oh, no, we don't want to put you out," they say, carrying their things into the guest room.

"Mom, you're not putting me out," I say. "There's a lot more room in my bedroom."

"We'll be all right," they insist. They've completely filled up the guest bedroom and are now unloading their stuff in the living room. It begins to look like a marshaling yard for the D-Day invasion.

"I'd rather have you upstairs," I plead. By now, the entire downstairs is packed with their paraphernalia. But it's a tradition. They always stay in the guest bedroom. I don't know why.

Maybe there are fewer fleas.

Game #4: Moving my furniture.

The third routine my parents go through is rearranging my furniture. My dad puts on his work clothes and moves my living room furniture around while my mother sits on the couch and gives him directions.

"Try the TV set over there, Fred," she'll say. "A little more to the left." "More to the left." "Back to the right a little." "That's good." I sit on the ottoman and watch. Nobody asks for my opinion. After they leave, it takes days to put everything back in its place.

Game #5: What's to eat?

My parents and I have nothing in common when it comes to food. I truly believe I am adopted. I eat tofu and fresh vegetables. My parents, when traveling, give themselves permission to eat massive amounts of junk food. Since they know I don't keep junk food around the house, they bring their own. After politely struggling to swallow my tofu and fresh vegetables, they get out the peanuts, pretzels, potato chips, nacho chips, cheese doodles, and party mix and watch TV. In its new position.

Right before bed, while eating large bowls of ice cream, they decide that the television set should be in a new spot.

Game #6: How can we help Sally?

Whenever they visit, my parents walk around my house and make a list of the things they think I need. Then they take me to the hardware to help me buy the stuff (a new garbage can, a "welcome" doormat, a set of screwdrivers I'll never use). This would be great if it wasn't for the fact that they expect me to pay for it. This is their way of helping. I get stuff they like at my expense. I was surprised the first time this happened, but now I'm used to it.

I'm not the only one who has trouble with visits from parents.

One of my girlfriends had her in-laws from Belgium for five weeks one summer. They didn't rearrange her furniture, but they tinkered with almost everything else, from the temperature on the hot water heater to the heat settings on the washer and dryer.

Before going to bed one evening, they decided to turn on the air conditioning. Unfortunately, they hit the wrong button. In the middle of the night, everyone woke to the smell of smoke. Yelling "Fire!" they all met in the hallway in various stages of dress before realizing the furnace was on full force.

Let me set the record straight. I adore my parents. I love their visits. I wouldn't trade them for anything.

Plus, they never criticize me about my housecleaning. Whenever my friend Terri's mom comes to visit, the first thing her mom does is run her fingers across the top of the refrigerator to check for dust.

Family Reunions

My family thinks I should be in charge of our family reunions. I guess they think I have more time than they do. (Yeah, right.) Or, maybe it's because I'm the writer in the family. In any event, to date, I've organized four of our family reunions and executed the job as cheerfully as possible.

If your family doesn't hold reunions, you're welcome to attend one of ours. But first, let me describe the highlights of our last reunion.

THE INVITATION

TO: Members of the Richardson family
FROM: The Reunion Planning Committee (Me, Sally
    Coffman)
RE: Reunion Update

Greetings and salutations family members currently residing on this planet. Plans for the reunion at Shirley and Roger's on July 4th are progressing at great speed—well, at least we have the date—and I wanted to give everyone an update as to where we are at present. To begin with, let me clue you in about the location.

THE LOCATION

Cousin Shirley and her husband Roger have graciously agreed to host the reunion at their country estate in northeastern Ohio (aka their farm). If you're coming in your camper, you'll have a field in which to park and access to several port-a-potties. There's also a motel in town (Motel 4). It was built in the early '50s and hasn't been remodeled since then, so it's . . . well . . . rather rustic. The rooms have wood paneling on the walls (and ceilings) and the bathrooms have sliding wood doors, which don't close, if that tells you anything.

THE FOOD

Shirley and Roger have figured out menus for three meals on Saturday and believe they can feed everyone for $10.00 per person. I, for one, think this is a great idea and that we should take them up on it before they decide to back out. You're probably all getting big checks back from the IRS at this time of year (ha ha!) so why don't you go ahead and send your personal check to Shirley before you spend it all. Actually, if we send the money ahead of time, she can buy supplies on sale. A family of four would send a check for $40.00 etc. etc. etc. If you don't send a check ahead of time, you won't receive a map showing where the reunion is going to be.

WHAT TO BRING

Plan to bring: bathing suits, towels, softball equipment (Shirley has a ball and bat), tennis equipment (if you want to play tennis), and golf clubs (if you want to play golf). Bridge tables will be set up inside the house for those who want to play bridge, and beds will be available for those who need (or want) to take naps.

THE AGENDA

Friday night. Shirley has invited us to sit around the pool on Friday night when we get in. Stop by and let us know you've arrived. Then, you'll need to get a good night's sleep, because . .

Saturday is Orienteering Day! We'll meet around 8 a.m., have breakfast, then everyone will be assigned to a team exercise. We're taking volunteers for people to be on Joey's team. Those of you who attended the last reunion may remember the trouble we had with Joey moving some of the clues so the other teams couldn't find them. Because of that, we're asking Joey to give a short lecture on ethics prior to the Orienteering exercise, hoping that that will get him into the correct frame of mind.

The highlight of Saturday evening will be a bonfire complete with singing and family stories. Please bring a family story (or tall tale) to tell. A prize will be given for the most creative piece of entertainment! This is your chance to show off your dramatic talents and/or your talent cooking hotdogs on a stick.

COMMITTEES

The "cousins" have each been assigned to a committee. Please find your name in the list below. If you'd like to get out of the committee you've been assigned to, you may do so IF you can find someone to switch with and IF you do so before May 1st. Questions about how the committees were assigned should be kept to yourself.

Invitations: Sally
Sleeping Arrangements, Housing: Becky Lynn
      (Before sleeping with someone, make sure you are
      with the correct person in the correct bed)
Food: Shirley and Roger
Security and Parking: Joey
Entertainment, Organized Activities, Sports: Crazy Uncle Al
Just Getting Themselves There: Buddy, Earl
Emergency Loans, Financial Aid: Fred
All-around, General Advice on What's Going Wrong: Aunt Minnie
Morning Calisthenics, Supervised Hiking and Jogging: Denny Lou
Getting Everyone to Laugh by Telling Her Various Life Adventures: Katie
Campfire Stories: Aunt Jenny
Credit For The Idea of Having a Family Reunion
(And Person to Hold Responsible If It's a Fiasco):   Buddy
Inter-Family Communications: Jackson
Settling Disputes (Adult Disputes Only):   Mary Kay
      (the Kids Will Have to Work Things Out Themselves)

Evaluating the Reunion and Deciding If It Should Ever Be Held Again: Fern
Writing a Follow-up Report: Leftie

THE AFTERMATH

The reunion did, indeed, take place the weekend of July 4th
and was deemed a huge success. Being the writer that I am, I feel
compelled to submit the following report based on my personal
observations and interviews with the attendees.

NOTES FROM THE EVALUATION COMMITTEE AND SUGGESTIONS FOR FUTURE REUNIONS

1. It's been suggested—and I agree—that we should take the
group photo at the beginning of the reunion (when we're all
happy to see each other) rather than at the end. (See attached
photo.)
2. We're sorry that Katie's friend Randy sprained his ankle
playing tennis and had to spend the day at Urgent Care. Even
though nobody got to meet him, we're sure he's a wonderful
guy. (He's the guy in the picture on crutches.)
3. In the future, the first aid kit will include calamine lotion. I
know most of you were not expecting the abundance of poison
ivy in the woods when you were chasing balls in the outfield
during the baseball game.
4. Speaking of the baseball game, there is still some question
about whether Mary Kay, while pitching, deliberately hit Joey,
who was batting. According to Mary Kay, it was an accident.
According to Joey, it was deliberate. According to the majority

of the bystanders, Mary Kay had every right to "make Joey pay" since Mary Kay's son Alex was on Joey's orienteering team and Joey took off and left Alex behind so he could win. Joey: one does not leave a five-year-old crying in the back pasture by himself. It's also been suggested that in the future we have an umpire to officiate the game. I wasn't there, but I understand there was some disagreement over the words "ball," "strike," "foul," "safe," and "out."

5.   The food committee apologizes about the cookout. Next time, the golfers need to call and inform us if they decide to play 18 holes instead of nine. By the time they returned, the hamburgers were cold and the potato salad was hot. Sorry, sorry, sorry if you were one of the people who got sick.

6.   Under no circumstances, will politics EVER be discussed at a reunion again.

7.   Some of you spent time showing others what you had in the trunks of your cars. What was that all about?

8.   The littler kids were pretty traumatized by the frogs in the swimming pool. If you have older kids, next year you MUST keep them from collecting frogs and throwing them into the pool.

9.   As far as the food on Sunday is concerned, everyone agrees that trying to order fast food was a fiasco. The hamburger people refused to vote for pizza. The pizza eaters refused to consider Chinese. The Chinese food people gagged at the thought of fried chicken. It ended up not mattering since nobody wanted to collect the money and go for the food anyway. I think we need a committee to investigate a better plan for next year.

10. Speaking of next year, plans are a bit tenuous. As I was saying "goodbye" to each of you, I asked if there was any interest in having a reunion again next year. Many of you said you had other plans, which I thought was strange since I hadn't mentioned a date.

11. Anyway, if there IS interest in another reunion and you'd like me to help out, you can reach me at:

forgetitI'mnevergoingtodothisagain.com
Sally Coffman

Reflections on My Childhood

When I have a bad day and everything seems to be going wrong, I catch myself wishing I could go home. Not to the home I live in now, but to the house on Claire Avenue where I grew up with my parents, my brother, and my sister. For just a few hours, I'd like to be a little girl again without any responsibilities.

Here's what I would do:

I'd sit in front of the hot air register on a cold winter evening and soak up all the heat. I'd call my best friend Vickie on our old black telephone with the heavy receiver and giggle all night long.

I'd wake up on Christmas morning and run downstairs to see the presents under the tree. I'd jump on my bicycle on the first day of spring and ride as fast as I could. I'd clean out my locker on the last day of school knowing that summer vacation would last forever.

I'd spend a day with Travis, my brother's best friend, who quickly became my best friend. Travis spent so much time at our house that when we moved away, we told the buyers that he came with the house.

I'd stuff my bra with Kleenex again so I'd have something to show. I'd relive that once-in-a-lifetime experience when my mom took me downtown on the bus and bought me my first pair of heels.

I'd go back and relive one of those Sunday mornings when our family was leaving for church, and my cat Impy would escape out the back door. We'd all scatter in different directions to try to catch her. I'd stand there crying: "We can't go to church until we find her!" while my dad would tell us to leave the cat and get into the car. (We always caught her in time.)

I'd want to feel that feeling I had when I realized Tim from my church group could be thinking about me at the same time I was thinking about him.

Just once more, I want Kent to give me a ride home after the basketball game where he scored 25 points. I want to pass notes in math class. I want to go to a football game on the pep bus and kiss Jimmy the whole way home. I want to go back to my senior prom.

Just once more, I'd like to wake up to the sound of the shower running and know that my Dad is getting ready for work and that all is right in the world. I want to back the car down the driveway and up our neighbor's tree like I did the first time my Dad took me driving, just so I can see the look on his face again. I want my Dad to come to my ballet recital. And to warm the car up for me when it's cold.

I want my Mom to make a bed for me on the couch when I'm sick and treat me like I'm the most important person in the world. I want her to stand nearby and help me learn new things, like she did when I was learning to put my contact lenses in. I want her to make waffles. And to praise me when I master a new piece on the piano.

I know these are only memories and that I can never actually do any of these things again. But when I reminisce, an amazing thing happens. I realize what a beautiful childhood I had, and how very, very much I was loved.

And that's what gets me through the bad times.

Shopping at Macy's (Part I)

I've always been fascinated by kids. Several of my girlfriends have kids and I enjoy playing different roles in their lives, such as Aunt, babysitter, and tutor. As an Aunt, I buy them annoying, noisy toys to drive their mothers crazy. As a babysitter, I try to follow the directions on the frozen TV dinners and keep the dogs from eating the furniture. And, as a teacher, I do homework with them. But until Hannah came along, I'd never tried taking any of them shopping.

Hannah is the youngest daughter of my good friend Linda. Even though Linda makes a good salary, she usually shops at Wal-Mart because she can get more for her money. Now, Hannah is a clothes horse. She wears only the latest fashions. So, for her eighth birthday, instead of buying her something myself, I thought it would be fun to take her to Macy's. Every young girl needs to experience Macy's.

What was particularly appealing about this idea was that not only would I have the fun of shopping with Hannah, I'd be able to pull a fast one on Linda. Once Hannah had sampled Macy's, she'd never want to go back to Wal-Mart. Ha! Ha! (It was an evil plan. But that's what friends are for.)

When I picked Hannah up to take her to the mall, I could tell she was really psyched. It occurred to me that it might be a good idea if I set some boundaries. I figured I could afford a cute top—on sale. So, on our way to Macy's, I started preparing her. I explained that we were going to buy "One top. On sale." I repeated myself. "One top. On sale." I made her repeat it too. "One top. On sale."

As I predicted, Hannah fell in love with Macy's. She studied the outfits on the manikins. She looked in all the display cases. We stopped at the cosmetic counter and tried on different perfumes. Then we arrived at our destination—the girl's department. And we began shopping.

Hannah's arms quickly filled with clothes she wanted to try on. My arms filled with clothes she wanted to try on. When we couldn't carry any more, we found a dressing room and started in. If there was something she liked, but we didn't have the right size, I'd go and get a different size. I'd never experienced this before. It was great! We were shopping!

Eventually we narrowed the field to the five items she liked best. (None of which were "One top. On sale.") The point was, we were having a good time.

After about an hour and a half, I said: "Okay, Hannah, you need to pick one."

"But I like them all."

"I'm sure you do. But you can only have one."

"Why?"

"Because I only have money for one."

"Don't you have a checkbook?"

"Yes, but I'm not going to use it."

"Why not?"

"Because we already agreed you can only buy one thing."

"Why?"

"Because I don't have enough money for more than one thing."

"Do you have a credit card?"

"I do, but I'm not going to use it."

"Why not?"

"Because our deal was to buy "One top. On sale. " Remember? You're going to have to choose one."

"Let's call my mother."

"Why would we call your mother?"

"Maybe she could put the dress on her credit card."

"No, we're not going to call your mother. Pick one."

After trying everything on again, Hannah got it down to two items.

"Okay, Hannah. Pick one." We'd now been at the store for almost two hours. Mothers and daughters were lined up to use the dressing room.

"I like them both."

"I'm sure you do. But you have to pick one."

"Couldn't we buy this one today, and you could buy the other one and give it to me for Christmas?"

"No. Pick one. I like the black culottes. They make a lot of sense. You could wear them with lots of different things."

"But I like the dress."

"Okay. Then let's get the dress."

"But I like the culottes. Couldn't I have them both? I want them both. Pleeeze. . . "

I was tired. I was hungry. I was never going to convince her of the concept of "one."

"We're going to buy these," I said, making an executive decision. I grabbed the culottes and took them to the register. There was just one thing I hadn't checked. The price. They were about three times what I was planning to spend. How could a pair of culottes for an eight-year-old cost that much? But I was tired. I was hungry. I had a little girl who didn't understand why I wouldn't buy her the two . . . no, the five, pieces of clothing.

I pulled out my credit card and charged the pants. I suddenly realized my plan to pull a fast one on Linda had backfired. I'd ended up pimping myself.

Linda "Oohed" and "Aahed" at the culottes when we got home. Hannah ran off to put them on and go play. They weren't the kind of culottes you'd play in! Linda gave me a hug and walked me to the door.

"You look beat," she said. "Maybe you should go home and take a nap."

Which I did.

In retrospect, I did accomplish what I'd set out to do. Hannah now knows what Macy's is and asks her mother to go there on a regular basis.

I, however, am still walking around mumbling "One top. On sale" and trying to figure out where I went wrong.

Shopping at Macy's (Part II)

Linda raised her eyebrows.

"Are you sure you're up to it?"

She was referring to my offer to take her two daughters shopping for a Mother's Day present.

Six months had passed since I'd taken Hannah, her youngest daughter, to Macy's and spent my life savings on the pair of culottes she wanted. I'd learned a lot from that experience. I was not going to make that mistake twice. I assured Linda that if Bailee and Hannah and I went shopping, we'd use their money, not mine.

After Linda gave me her blessing (and wished me luck), I took the girls aside and offered to take them to the mall that weekend to get their mom a present. I made it clear we'd only go to one store, shop only for their mother, and use their money. During the week, I reminded the girls several times to get their money together. After all, their mom was special. Their mom always bought them presents. Wouldn't it be great to see their mom's face when she opened presents from them?

The day of our shopping trip arrived and I went to pick them up. Bailee, the 12-year-old, buckled herself into the passenger's seat, while Hannah, the eight-year old buckled herself into the back seat. Before we pulled out of the driveway, we had a talk.

"Remember, we're only going to one store," I said.

They nodded.

"Where do you want to go?"

"Macy's!" they both cried.

"Okay. How much money do you each have?"

"Thirty dollars," Hannah said smugly.

"Good. Bailee, how much money do you have?"

"I don't have any."

"What do you mean, you don't have any? Don't you get an allowance?"

"Yes."

"Well, why didn't you bring your allowance?"

"My mom keeps it for us."

"But you don't have any money with you now?" I repeated. "Bailee, this is for your mother. She does so much for you. She makes all sorts of sacrifices for you." How much do you chew a 12-year-old out? I paused. "So, what are we going to do?"

"I could loan her some of my money," Hannah said cheerfully.

"That would work. How much money would you be willing to loan her?"

"Ten dollars," Hannah said, handing her sister one of her three $10 bills.

"Okay. Bailee, when we get home, do you have ten dollars to repay your sister?"

"Yes."

"So, when we get home, you need to go get the ten dollars and pay your sister back. Okay?"

"Okay." The deal struck, we started off.

Linda had said she wanted earrings, so at Macy's, we headed to the jewelry department. At the first counter, there was a beautiful strand of blue pearls that I knew Linda would like. I pointed it out to the girls. The necklace was $30.00. If they pooled their money, they could get it. They didn't want to do that. They each wanted to get their mother something on their own.

Okay. I was all right with that. We started browsing.

After a few minutes, Hannah (who, remember, has $20.00) couldn't find anything she liked, so she decided she wanted to go back and get the $30.00 pearls. She asked if I'd go in with her.

"No. Keep looking."

Hannah then found some earrings with dolphins on them. We don't have a lot of dolphins in Indiana, but if that's what she wanted, it was fine with me. The earrings were $25.00. When I told her she couldn't afford them. she began to pout.

At that point, I realized we were missing Bailee.

"Where's your sister?" I asked in a panic. Macy's jewelry department was huge. I'd lost Bailee. I'd assumed the three of us were going to stay together. Off we went to find Bailee. She was in the upscale jewelry section, picking up and handling all the jewelry that she could. Oh, great. We were going to be arrested for shop-lifting. I explained to Bailee that we had to stay together. And that she shouldn't touch anything.

It's now occurred to Hannah that she could afford the dolphin earrings if Bailee would give her back the money she'd loaned her.

Bailee said "no."

At which point, Hannah started to cry. "I want to get her the dolphin earrings!"

I tried to point out that: (1) her mother had never shown any real interest in dolphins, and (2) that there was a lot of other jewelry we hadn't seen yet that might be even better than the dolphin earrings. While I was trying to calm her down (everyone was looking at us), I looked around for Bailee. We'd lost Bailee again. Oh, great. I knew it. She'd been picked up for shop-lifting. Wouldn't that make a lovely Mother's Day present—having to call Linda from jail and asking her to come and bail us out?

Then the angels descended from heaven. Bailee found a lovely pair of earrings for $10.00. The saleslady (who'd been following us around) excused herself and said she was going to check on something. She came back and said she could discount the dolphin earrings from $25.00 to $20.00. Clearly, she wanted to get rid of us.

Hannah then decided that if the lady would discount the dolphins, maybe she'd discount the blue pearls. At that point, I grabbed the two $10.00 bills from her hand and gave them to the clerk.

Mission accomplished. We headed back to the car.

As the girls started texting on their cell phones, I grinned and patted myself on the back. We'd gotten two presents, Hannah had stopped crying, nobody had been arrested for shop-lifting, and all I had to pay out of my own pocket was the tax. Linda was going to have to eat her words – accusing me of not being able to take the girls shopping.

As soon as I got the girls home, I turned to Bailee and said:

"You need to go right now and pay your sister back the ten dollars."

Linda asked what was going on.

"Bailee didn't have any money, so Hannah loaned her ten dollars of her money."

And that's when I discovered my fatal flaw. Linda said:

"But I gave Hannah the thirty dollars for both of them."

I went home and cried.

Lessons From My Cats

A guy I was dating once told me I had to choose between him and my cats. I chose my cats. At the time, my motto was: "Men are a Dime a Dozen, but a Good Cat is Hard to Find." (Which isn't true. All cats are good cats.) In any event, I now ask "Do you like cats?" when I meet someone for the first time.

Both men—and cats—have taught me a lot about life. Here are some things I've learned from my cats:

1. Communication is the key to any good relationship.

Cats thrive on communication. You must talk to a cat. The more you talk to them, the more their personalities emerge, and the closer the two of you will become. I have a friend who doesn't interact with her cat. She says her cat doesn't like to be touched, but when I visit, I get down on the floor, roll the cat over on her back, rub her tummy, and tell her how beautiful she is. What cat doesn't like to hear that?

In his best-selling book *Outliers*, Malcolm Gladwell tells of a town in Pennsylvania where the residents live to ripe old ages—

without suffering major diseases. The reason? According to the researchers, it was because people talked to each other. During the day, the men talked at work; in the evenings, the families visited with their neighbors.

Cats have always known that talking is healthy.

2. If you want your ears washed, you have to be willing to wash someone else's.

I love watching my Tonkinese, Egg Foo Young, put his arms around our Siamese kitten, Tuey, and wash the inside of her ears. She then reciprocates. This is a great life lesson. My dad, a good Methodist, always got people who moved into our neighborhood to go to our church. He started by finding out what was important to them. For example, when the Shuberts moved in across from us, my dad discovered that Mr. Shubert owned the local gas station.

Guess where we started to buy gas?

Guess who started coming to church?

3. Go with the flow.

When I was growing up, my parents wouldn't let us have a family pet. My mother's objection: she didn't want to clean cat (or dog) hair off the furniture. But when I was 10 years old, I entered a contest in the *Cleveland Plain Dealer* and won a pedigreed seal-point Siamese kitten. My parents would have looked like schmucks if they'd refused to let me have the kitten, so our family suddenly had a cat. Impy.

Surprisingly, the issue of Impy's shedding never came up. I

discovered why when I came home from school one day and found my mother holding her by the neck with one hand, and vacuuming her with the hose on the vacuum cleaner with the other. The old, round, brown vacuum was making a hell of a racket, but Impy just hung there patiently. Obviously she'd figured out that if she was going to be a member of our family, she'd have to put up with being vacuumed.

In life, there are similar occasions when you have to just "go with the flow" and not fight your situation. Sometimes you need to do things you're not happy about doing, knowing that by doing so, it will get you closer to an even bigger goal.

4. If you lean against the screen in the upstairs window, you might fall out. But you'll probably land on your feet and have a great story to tell.

Last summer, I noticed that the screen in one of my upstairs windows was loose. A little voice in my head said: "Hmm. I wonder if Tuey could fall out." Then a second little voice said: "That's ridiculous. Tuey can't fall out." This debate continued inside my head for about a week.

Then I attended an overnight conference. When I returned home, only Foo Young showed up to greet me. He didn't seem upset that she was gone; he just wanted his breakfast.

I could hear a faint "meow," so I threw down my overnight case and started racing through the house. I thought: "She's in a drawer. Or a closet. Or she fell and broke her leg." I kept yelling: "Hang on, Tuey, Mommy's coming," but I couldn't find her.

Then I looked out my back door. There was a beautiful Siamese cat with her front feet up on the door.

"That's a beautiful cat," I thought.

"That cat looks a lot like my cat."

"That is my cat!"

I have no idea how long she was outside, but by the way she pranced around all day, I could tell she was proud of herself. She probably hadn't meant to fall out of the window, but she'd obviously made the best of the situation.

I had a similar adventure one time when I had an invitation to tour a nuclear submarine. When I accepted the invitation, I assumed there'd be a staircase to get down into the boat. When I arrived, there was just a ladder. I screamed the whole way down, but was proud of myself once I made it. And when I got back on dry land, I pranced around like Tuey did.

Someone once said you should try something scary every day. I don't think my heart could take that. But I do believe that, occasionally, you should do things that are scary.

5. Eat slowly and savor every bite.

No, wait. That's giraffes. Or camels. Or cows.

No normal cat eats slowly. Egg Foo Young snarfs his food so fast that when I got Tuey, I put her breakfast up on the kitchen counter rather than on the floor with his. Then I'd go in the bedroom and get ready for work. When I returned, both bowls were empty. I eventually realized that as soon as I'd left the kitchen, he'd jump up and eat her breakfast, then jump back down to finish his.

I've tried to explain to him that food tastes better when you chew it, but my words fall on deaf ears.

Incidentally, chewing slowly does make food taste better.

6. If there's something you really want, be persistent.

Have you ever watched a cat lying in wait to catch a mouse? Now, that's persistence. Here are some of my cats' conversations that demonstrate persistence:

"Excuse me. I'm ready to sit on your lap. Oh, you're reading the newspaper (using your laptop, eating your breakfast)? How does that affect me? I want to sit on your lap." (Repeat until he gets what he wants.)

"Excuse me. It's supper time. I'd like my dinner. You want me to wait? How long do you want me to wait? (Repeat until he gets what he wants.)

"Hold it. That's the cat food *you* want me to eat. I want the really expensive kind. If you try to feed me this, I'm going to just sit and stare at you. Oh, and it needs to be a fresh can. I want to hear the seal being broken and the lid being pulled off. Don't expect me to eat it cold, out of the refrigerator. And don't think you can fool me by microwaving it." (Repeat until he gets what he wants.)

I once dated a guy who played bridge and wanted me to learn so we could join a bridge club together. So, I took lessons at the local YMCA. When I started, I barely knew that a "10" was higher than a "9." And I had no clue what a Jack, Queen, King, or Ace were. So I struggled. There was so much to learn, and it was so frustrating, that after each class, I'd lock myself in my car and cry for about five minutes before I could drive home.

I stuck with it, though, and now play bridge once a week. In fact, bridge is one of the great pleasures in my life.

7. Always look like you're paying attention, even when you're bored.

This tip is especially useful in staff meetings.
And in college classrooms. I believe instructors should always try to look like they're paying attention.

8. Make sure people notice you.

Tuey can't stand it when I give Foo Young my full attention. In the evening, when I'm lounging in my Lazy-Boy chair with Foo Young on my lap, she:

Leaps from on top of the piano onto Foo Young like a kamikaze pilot.
Jumps onto a piece of tissue paper and slides across the hardwood floor like it's a skate board.
Puts toys in the food bowl so Foo Young can't get to his food.

Actually, Tuey's enthusiasm and desire to make people notice her are great strategies for life. People are attracted to cats—and other people—who are happy and enthusiastic.

When I turned 15, I was allowed to start double-dating. There were plenty of girls in my class, so I needed to do something to stand out. I learned to say "Coffman's!" when I answered the phone so guys would remember me and want to call back.

9. Head butting will get you farther than hissing will.

Your mother probably told you the old adage "you can catch more flies with honey than with vinegar." It's true. You need to learn to get what you want in life through reasoning and good manners rather than by bullying or being aggressive. And to try to resolve problems before they get to the "hissing" stage. (Note: some occasions do warrant hissing, like visits to the vet, or the introduction of a younger, cuter, or more cuddly animal in the house.)

10. Never laugh at someone who jumps and misses the chair.

Never, ever, ever laugh at a cat. Or at a sixth grader's band concert. My friend Diane once invited me to her daughter's sixth grade band concert. The kids had only had their instruments for about four weeks, so when the conductor raised his baton, the kids all played different notes at different speeds. It was the funniest thing I'd ever heard. I threw my head back and let out a loud laugh. The parents in the audience snapped their heads around and stared at me with daggers in their eyes. I crawled under my chair.

That's how I learned to never laugh at a sixth grader's band concert.

Never, ever, ever.

Well, those are the 10 things I've learned from my cats. Now, here's the most important lesson of all. It evolved from the fact that when I travel, I have different friends come in and feed my cats.

Be nice to everyone.

You never know who's going to feed you.

The Surprise Party

𝒟ear Diane:

Well, I had a close call last night. You know how I'm planning a surprise party for my friend Sam? Well, he almost discovered evidence of it. (Incidentally, the party is at his house. That's part of the surprise.) Anyway, I bought some soft drinks and decided to keep them in the trunk of my car rather than bring them into my house and then have to reload them into the car to take to his house. It's been plenty cold, so I knew they'd stay cold in the car.

Well, a couple of the bottles escaped from their bags and were rolling around in the trunk. Not a problem, since I'm the only one who drives my car.

But yesterday we went to Delphi for dinner and decided to take my car. Sam drove. Now, when he drives, he brakes suddenly, accelerates quickly, and turns corners fast. So the bottles started rolling around and making a racket. I turned the radio up real loud, and since his hearing's not that good, I figured he wouldn't hear them.

But he finally asked: "What's that noise in the trunk?"

I couldn't tell him the truth, so I tried to think of something believable to say. It sounded like barbells rolling around, so I said: "Barbells."

He always believes what I tell him, so I knew that would be the end of the conversation.

He thought for a minute, then said: "Why in the world would you have barbells in your trunk?"

I thought for a minute. No reason. So I laughed and said: "No. (Ha ha!) Actually, it's a bottle of coke."

He always believes what I tell him, so I knew that would be the end of the conversation.

He thought for a minute, then said: "You don't drink coke." Now, he never pays attention to my food habits, but this time he was right. I don't drink coke.

So I said: "Um. Oh, it's a bottle of Sprite. For Hannah."

He looked at me and said: "Huh?" I realized I was going to have to make up a longer story.

"The Sprite is for Hannah. You know. When I tutor her on Sundays."

"I don't get it." (Neither did I.) So I kept explaining. "You know I tutor Hannah after church. We always stop and get something to eat on our way to my house."

"I don't get it. You eat out with Hannah?"

(Shit, shit, shit.)

"No, Hannah and I stop to get something to eat on our way home. You know how I hate fast food. So I get her something to eat and I always have something to eat for myself at home."

"You don't get her a drink?"

"No," I said slowly, stalling. "I'm trying to teach her how

expensive it is to buy drinks at fast food places. So I told her I'd buy her a bottle of Sprite and keep it at my house."

Note to reader: There are a number of bottles of soft drinks in the trunk, none of which is a Sprite.

He thought for a minute, then said: "I still don't get it. Explain it to me again."

This has become the longest conversation Sam and I have ever had. I go through it again. Finally, I was able to change the subject.

I thought he'd forgotten about it . . . until we pulled onto my street and he brought it up again.

"It sounds like more than one bottle."

Shit, shit, shit. It's actually six bottles. I know he's going to look in the trunk when we get to my house. How am I going to explain the other five bottles?

I'm dying here. Trying to think of something to say to cover. If he offers to get "it" out of the trunk, I'm dead. If he suggests that I bring "it" in, I'd sound foolish if I said I'd rather keep it in the trunk. So my plan was to open the trunk really fast, pull out a bottle and yell: "I got it" and stick it under my coat.

When we got to my house, I gave him all sorts of things to carry in from the car so his hands would be full, and I started asking him questions about the basketball game we were going to watch. I think that distracted him. He didn't mention the bottle of "Sprite" any more. So, I don't think he caught on that I'm planning a party. We'll find out Sunday.

All I know is I'm not very good at lying. And I'm not going to plan any more surprise parties. They're really stressful.

Sally

CHALLENGES OF HOMEOWNERSHIP

Buying My First House

Once upon a time I lived in an apartment. I had central air, wall-to-wall carpeting, and a landlord who fixed whatever needed to be fixed. And I was happy. My friends, however, decided I'd be even happier if I bought a house. For privacy, they said. For income tax purposes. For a sense of security and well-being. So, I bought a house.

It's a quaint little cottage on a wooded lot on Oak Lane. To get there, you go down a gravel lane that looks like someone's driveway. The house has tall, cross-hatched windows, beautiful hardwood floors, and an attic that reminds me of the room I had when I was a little girl. I decided to make the attic my bedroom, where I could read novels on weekends and listen to the rain on the roof.

I've been in the house for more than a year now and have yet to read a novel while listening to the rain on the roof. Here's what I've been doing instead:

OCTOBER

DAY 1: Spent the day unpacking. While I was preheating the oven for dinner, the smoke alarm went off. Should the inside of an oven be black, I wondered, as I stuck my head in. Stopped what I was doing and made a trip to the store to buy oven cleaner. After cleaning it twice, I discovered the inside of the oven was not painted black.

Decided to take a shower to clean off the oven grease. After several minutes, noticed the water had filled the tub up half-way to my knees. Figured the drain handle was in the wrong position and changed it. Continued to shower. Noticed the water was now almost to the top of the tub. Discontinued shower. Got a screwdriver, unscrewed the drain cover, and pulled out a slimy, ten-foot-long hairball that looked like it belonged in a Vincent Price horror movie.

DAY 2: The handle on the toilet would not depress. Called the friends who talked me into buying the house to come over and fix it. They weren't home. Since this was the only toilet in the house, figured I'd better do something. Took the top off the toilet tank, reached in, and fished around until I found something loose. Pulled out a black, dog-eaten strap with a rusted safety pin on the end. Refastened the safety pin onto an appropriate-looking lever and spent the rest of the day cursing the previous owner and my friends.

DAY 5: My new bed arrived! No more sleeping on the couch! "Where do you want the bed, lady?" the delivery men asked. "Upstairs," I answered. The queen-sized box spring wouldn't bend enough to go up the 90 degree turn at the bottom of the stairs. "Now, where do you want the bed, lady?" "Upstairs," I repeated firmly, knowing the reason I bought this house was to lie in bed on weekends, read novels, and listen to the rain on the roof. After watching them struggle for another 20 minutes, I finally agreed the bed wouldn't fit up the stairs. We put it in the small bedroom downstairs. The downstairs bedroom is now wall-to-wall bed.

DAY 10: Came home from work and found my lawn covered with leaves—how exciting! My very own leaves! Changed my clothes and started raking. Used the back porch light and a flashlight after it got dark. Put "finish raking leaves" on tomorrow's list of things to do.

DAY 11: Got home from work, changed clothes, and started raking. Not as much fun as it was yesterday. Decided I needed help and called my friends who talked me into buying the house. "Come help me rake leaves," I demanded. "We have our own leaves," they said cheerfully. "Keep at it!" Made mental note never again to buy a house on a street named for a tree.

DAY 12: Saturday. "Finish raking leaves" was still on my list of things to do. I discovered that every time I removed a leaf from the lawn, a new one fell. Decided people never "finish raking leaves" and that I would just leave the lawn au naturelle.

NOVEMBER

It's below freezing and blustery cold. Pat and Gary called to ask if I needed help putting my storm windows in. "What are storm windows?" I asked. "We'll be right over." We spent a half-hour in the basement looking for storm windows. We didn't find any. "Good luck!" they hollered as they drove off. "What are storm windows?" I called back.

DECEMBER

Winter arrived. I discovered what storm windows are for. In my living room, the wind came in through the cracked, single-pane windows on the west side of the house, swirled around and gathered speed in the middle of the living room, and exited through the cracked windows on the east side of the house. I bought a stocking cap and wore it whenever I went into the living room.

JANUARY

I pulled a muscle while painting the bathroom ceiling. Developed my very first stiff neck. I looked like Quasimodo as I dragged my body into Urgent Care. "What happened?" the doctor asked. I told her I'd been working on my house. She nodded understandingly. She was a homeowner, too. Left with a neck brace, a muscle relaxant, and a pain killer.

MARCH

The doctor and I were becoming good friends. I saw her for a pulled muscle in my lower back. "What happened this time?" she asked. "I lifted a fifty-pound bag of peat moss out of my trunk." She nodded understandingly. She was a homeowner, too. Then she asked if I might be happier if I sold my house. I couldn't do that, I told her. My house was a source of happiness and well-being.

APRIL

Spring arrived! My cats and I decided to sun ourselves in the backyard. The cats promptly got fleas. My eyes began watering and my nose started running. The vet gave me something for the fleas. The doctor gave me something for my allergies. The cats and I decided to spend the rest of spring indoors.

JULY

My allergies having subsided, I decided to venture out into the yard again. I noticed there were large parts of the lawn that the previous owner's dog had torn up. I decided to plant grass. Nobody told me you don't plant grass in the middle of a drought. The new grass sprouted, saw there was no water, and quickly retreated back into the ground.

EPILOGUE

As I sit here at my kitchen table watching the grass die, the weeds grow, and the ants come in under the door, I can't help but remember my old apartment. I remember how I used to come home from work, pop dinner into the microwave, and spend my evenings with my feet up, watching TV. I don't think I'm cut out to be a homeowner. I think my cats and I were meant to find our happiness and well-being in an apartment.

I must admit that I am getting better at refastening the safety pin in the toilet. The trips to the doctor have tapered off, and I have ordered storm windows for next fall. Do you suppose this is how Mike Holmes got his start?

Painting My House

The paint was peeling. The color was fading. The boards were crying out for help. I couldn't ignore it any longer. It was time to paint my house.

After getting estimates from several painters, I realized I couldn't afford to have the house painted. I asked my friend Tom if he would paint it. He pointed out that he was in the process of painting his house.

So I decided to do the next best thing. I hired my 16-year-old nephew, Jackson.

When I ran the idea past my brother and sister-in-law (Jackson's parents), they pointed out the fact that neither Jackson nor I had ever painted a house before. On the other hand, it's a small house. They thought we could do it in just one weekend. So, we came up with a plan. I would paint the first story of the house (by standing on the ground), and Jackson would paint the second story (by standing on a ladder). As "the weekend" drew nearer, my friends told me I was making a huge mistake. Did I know how much teen-agers ate? they asked.

Looking back, I should have been more suspicious about my

brother and sister-in-law being so supportive. They even delivered Jackson to my house (they live three hours away). As I watched them drive away, I saw them holding their sides and doubled over in hysterical laughter. I couldn't tell if they thought we were the blind leading the blind or if they were congratulating themselves about the money they were going to save by not having to feed Jackson for three days.

FRIDAY NIGHT

Jackson and I prepare the house for painting. We clean out the gutters, wash the boards, and go to the grocery to get $40 worth of junk food. We also go next door to borrow a ladder from my neighbors. The husband and wife are in their driveway yelling at each other. The husband is trying to jump-start his wife's car which wouldn't start since she had left the lights on. In a pause in their fight, I ask if we could borrow their ladder. The husband grumbles: "It's in the garage" from under the hood of the car. We take that as a "yes" and retrieve the ladder.

SATURDAY MORNING

Six a.m. The weather forecast is for 90 degrees with 90% humidity. No one told me you don't paint when it's 90 degrees. I wake Jackson up and give him the report. He says: "90% humidity— that means rain. Guess we won't paint today." He turns over and pulls the covers up over his head. I tap him on the shoulder and say: "That means we start now."

After he devours a large part of the junk food, we convene on the back side of the house. I instruct him to paint slowly and carefully. We dip our brushes in the paint, raise them to the boards, and begin brushing back and forth. We're in the shade. Our spirits are high. It's even sort of fun. We can do this! We can paint the house!

Jackson impresses me with how well he handles the ladder. I, myself, am afraid of ladders. Not only can he paint right-handed, but left-handed as well. I ask him about this and he says if you can paint left-handed, you don't need to move the ladder as often. I never would have thought of that.

The highlight of the day is when Jackson, on the ladder painting the second story of the house, asks me to throw him the larger paintbrush. Full of wet paint. Now, I know better than to throw a wet paintbrush to someone on a ladder, so I refuse to throw it. Jackson assures me he'll catch it. I know better than to throw a wet paintbrush to someone on a ladder, so I refuse to throw it. Jackson assures me he'll catch it. Even though I know better than to throw a wet paintbrush to someone on a ladder, I go ahead and throw it. It goes half-way up, comes back down, and (and this part we didn't consider ahead of time), lands in a large pile of dirt and leaves. We now have to stop what we're doing and clean off the brush.

The junk food is gone by noon. I make a run to McDonald's for lunch. For dinner Jackson takes my car and goes to get a meat-lovers pizza. He brings me the bill—$11.00.

That evening my muscles begin to stiffen up. I take two aspirin. I had offered to pay Jackson by the hour. We'd worked 12 and one-half hours so far. Aargh! What if it takes us another 12 and a half hours? I'm up all night taking aspirin and worrying about what it's going to cost.

SUNDAY MORNING

During the night my joints have congealed. My elbows and knees won't bend. I manage to wiggle to the bottom of the bed and stand up like an ironing board. We must start painting. Jackson gets up and makes another trip to the grocery store for more junk food. While he's gone, with great determination, I throw the ladder up against the house, climb to the top, and start painting. No more of this carefully dipping the brush in the can and smoothing the paint onto the house. Today we're going to slap it on.

I paint with my right hand. I paint with my left. When my hands get tired, I put the brush between my teeth and move my head back and forth. We are going to finish painting this house.

Today Jackson and I are painting in the sun. We didn't know to keep the paint cans in the shade, so the paint has gotten so thick we can barely stir it. To make matters worse, the house has grown considerably in size. And my brush is heavier. This couldn't be the brush I used yesterday. I begin to hallucinate. I dream I'm on a boat on Lake Michigan with the sun beating down on me. The boat starts to sink. I have to bail water to keep it afloat. I'm sinking! I'm sinking! I have to bail! Bail!

I return to reality. I'm standing in my flower bed painting my house in 90 degree heat. Please! Please! Put me back on the sinking boat!

Four p.m. By some miracle, we've finished. The only thing left is to put things away. I ask Jackson to clean my expensive, new brushes. He suggests we throw them away. Through gritted teeth, I tell him that's not going to happen. We return the neighbor's ladder.

I have a big "Thank you" speech prepared, but decide not to use it when he shows up at the door in his pajamas.

Jackson and I stand and look at the house. It looks great. I now have a newly-painted house, barely had to tap into my retirement fund, and am still speaking to my nephew.

Tom stops by to look at the house.

"Looks good. Of course, it would look even better with a second coat."

I pour the remaining paint over his head.

Feeding the Squirrels

I believe there are five stages of homeownership—shock, denial, anger, depression, and acceptance. You probably recognize them. They're the same five stages people go through when they're grieving. The way it works is, when you finally reach the highest level of homeownership—acceptance—there's inevitably another crisis that sets you back to stage one—shock—and you get to go through all five stages again.

My latest battle: squirrels.

It all started the evening J.R. came over to grill hamburgers in the backyard.

"You know what you need?" he asked, flipping a burger.

"What?" I replied cautiously, knowing that men are great at suggesting projects, but not always there for the follow-through.

"A bird feeder! With all these trees," he said, waving his spatula, "I'll bet you'd get finches, cardinals, tit mice . . ." He rattled off a list of birds, none of which sounded familiar. He said it was fun watching birds eating from a feeder. You could learn their habits. You could appreciate how delicate they were. Best of all, watching birds was relaxing. His enthusiasm was contagious. Maybe it was time I learned about birds.

I asked if he'd help me.

"Sure."

So we made a date the next day to go look at bird feeders.

DAY 1: J.R. arrives in his truck to take me to the hardware store. He helps me select a bird feeder, a giant bag of sunflower seeds, a garbage can to house the seeds, a shepherd's hook, and a bird book so I can learn to identify the different types of birds. We return home, mount the feeder in the backyard, and sit on the patio to wait for our first customer. The first customer is a large, gray squirrel. He shimmies up the shepherd's hook, hangs upside down by his tail, reaches his hand into one of the holes of the bird feeder, and stuffs his mouth full of sunflower seeds.

We shoo him away.

DAY 2: I jump out of bed and rush to the window to see what birds are on the feeder. There are no birds on the feeder. Yet the feeder is empty. I refill it. Several times. I finally realize the more I refill it, the more squirrels there are in the backyard. This new batch of squirrels includes an instructor who is teaching the others how to chew the plastic inserts in the bird feeder so the holes will be big enough for the sunflower seeds to just pour out onto the ground.

Tomorrow I will put an end to this freeloading. I intend to feed the birds, not the squirrels.

DAY 3: Second visit to the hardware store. This time, I buy an expensive, heavy-duty metal feeder, guaranteed to be squirrel-proof. At home, I discover the squirrels like this feeder even better than the plastic one because they feel more secure when they're hanging upside down. I take comfort in the fact that at least they aren't enlarging the holes.

DAY 4: I finally see my first bird—a blue jay, lying dead on the patio. I have no idea what he died of. Probably hunger. I get out my shovel, scoop him up, and put him in the garbage can.

I discuss my squirrel problem that evening with J.R. He suggests I put up a squirrel feeder on the opposite side of the patio so the squirrels will leave the bird food alone. We go to the hardware store and buy a squirrel feeder. That makes things much worse. The squirrels now have TWO places to eat.

DAY 7: While mowing the grass, I happen to glance up at the back of my house. Somebody has pulled up two of my gutter guards to make an entrance into the gutter. And there are pieces of shingle on the ground! It's one thing for the squirrels to eat the bird food— it's another for them to eat my house. I march inside and call J.R. Is he home? Of course not.

I call the humane society. They tell me to put ammonia-soaked rags and daisy wheels on the roof to discourage the varmints. My fourth trip to the hardware. Do you know how hard it is to find daisy wheels in August? In August, the stores are putting out their Christmas decorations. I could easily have bought a Christmas tree, but there were no daisy wheels. I settle for ammonia-soaked rags.

I return home, throw a ladder up against the house, and crawl up to inspect the damage. On my way up the ladder, a mosquito bites my left eyelid. By the time I reach the top, my eye has swollen shut. With my remaining eye, I peer into the gutter. I see what looks like the start of a nest. Somebody has been thinking about building a nest. Swallowing my disgust at having to put my hand into a filthy gutter that's over my head and that I can't see into, I reach in and begin cleaning it out.

It's going fine until something starts scurrying towards my hand. I descend the ladder screaming. Now I'm really mad. I'm now willing to pay someone to get rid of the squirrels.

Exterminators don't do squirrels, they inform me.

I call the humane society again. This time they suggest I set a trap to catch the squirrels. How can I do that? There are dozens of squirrels in my backyard. No birds. There have never been any birds.

I decide it's time to get out of the bird feeding business.

I pull the feeder out of the ground and throw it in the trash. I would have liked to have fed some birds, but as a homeowner, my first duty is to my house.

One thing I'm sure of: the squirrels won't do any further damage to my roof or my gutters.

That's where J.R.'s going to sleep for the next few weeks.

HOBBIES AND OTHER DISASTERS

Audition Forms

I love acting. The thing I don't like is filling out audition forms.

In the last few shows I've been in (in our local Community Theatre), the skills I was called upon to perform as an actress had nothing to do with the skills I was asked about on my audition form. For example, as Louise Jamison in a production of *Guilty Conscience* I had to fall down a set of stairs and die (one time), die from a gunshot wound (two times), go back and forth from short hair to long hair (four times), and change costumes in the dark in less than sixty seconds (six times). The audition form asked if I could sing, dance, or play a musical instrument.

As a matter of fact, I can sing, dance, and play a musical instrument. But my skills as a pianist gave me no insight about dying from a gunshot wound in the chest. What the audition form should have asked was: "Can you crumple gracefully and lie still for long periods of time without breathing?"

Not only would my answer ("No") have alerted the director that I have no experience dying, but I would have had a better idea of what I was getting myself into. At the audition I could have asked:

"Incidentally, where is this character going to die?" And if the director had answered truthfully: "On a flight of uncarpeted stairs," I could have excused myself and gone home to feed my cats.

(Eventually, I did learn to crumple gracefully on the uncarpeted stairs. And eventually, my bruises did go away.)

As I lay dead on the floor rehearsal after rehearsal, I had plenty of time to think about the questions I would ask if I were designing an audition form. Instead of asking people about their previous theatre experience, I would ask them about their means of transportation, their willingness to move heavy scenery, and how many tickets their family members would buy.

I'd also question the people auditioning about their wardrobes. My experience with productions has always been this: The week before the show opens, the costumer (who has finally shown up for the first time), says to the cast: "Why don't you all bring in something from home?" Then, of course, she disappears, never to be heard from again. Sometimes this works, especially if the play is set in the current time-period. Unfortunately, this costuming technique is frequently used for period pieces as well.

As Louise Jamison, I was expected to dress like the wife of an extremely wealthy New York attorney. My wardrobe, unfortunately, reflects the fact that I buy my clothes at J. C. Penney's at the mall in Lafayette, Indiana. "Fine." "Fine." "Fine." The director said about the clothes everyone else in the cast brought in. "Do you have anything . . . better?" she said when I showed her mine.

Why hadn't they asked at the audition what kind of clothes I had?

I also think audition forms should take the theatre—as well

as the play being produced—into account. In my high school, our only toilet had a habit of backing up, usually ten minutes before the curtain was to go up. We had to always make sure we cast someone in the show who knew how to plunge toilets. There was one young man who was able to get parts in all of the productions because of his ability (and cheerful willingness) to plunge.

What I'm trying to say is this: directors should not ask: "Can you do a British accent?" when what they really want is someone who can plunge a toilet.

To help clarify matters, both for directors casting shows and for actors auditioning for them, I've written a new audition form. If you or anyone you know in your theatre group is unhappy with the audition form you've been using and think this one might better suit your needs, please feel free to adopt it.

PROPOSED AUDITION FORM

Name: _____

Name of play: _____

Role you are auditioning for: _____

BIOGRAPHICAL DATA

Do you own (or have access to) a car? _____

How many miles does it have on it? _____

How well do you drive through snow? Ice? Sleet?_____

(Note: for those auditioning for winter shows, preference will be given to those with four-wheel drive vehicles.)

What is the general state of your health under pressure? _____

Do you function well without sleep? _____

Are you, or any members of your immediate family, planning to have a crisis in the next three months? Please explain. (Ask stage manager for additional paper if necessary.)

PREVIOUS THEATRE BACKGROUND

1. Which adjective best describes your feelings towards directors? I am:
    A. Openly hostile
    B. Inwardly hostile
    C. Usually able to ignore them
    D. All of the above
2. Which of the following best describes your feelings about the people helping backstage?
    A. You call that helping?
    B. I honestly try not to step on them
3. Which of the following best describes your feelings about your fellow actors?
    A. You call that acting?
    B. I honestly try not to step on them
    C. For the most part, especially onstage, I am usually able to ignore them
4. On a scale from 1 to 10, how important do you think it is for an actor to learn his/her lines exactly as they are written in the script?

1	2	3	4	5	6	7	8	9	10
Somewhat				Not Very				Somewhat	

5. In the past, have you been able to say your exact line even when your leading man/woman said the wrong line prior to yours, thus rendering your line meaningless?   YES   NO

6. Generally, how do you feel when you are onstage with no lines?
    A. I use the time to rest up until it's time to deliver my next line
    B. I use the time to think of my next line
    C. All of the above

7. Would you be willing to change your facial expression if someone you were in a scene with was doing something relatively dramatic? (e.g. choking to death, crying hysterically, begging you to spare their life, etc.)   YES   NO

8. Would you be willing to not change your facial expression if your leading man's fly came unzipped onstage?
                                                    YES   NO

9. Do you ever have the feeling that you'll know your lines if the curtain goes up at 8:00, but not if they hold the curtain until 8:05?
                                                    YES   NO

SPECIAL TALENTS
    1. Do you have access to a wide variety of clothes and period costumes your size?   YES   NO
    2. Would you be willing to bring all the furniture from your house in for use as the set?   YES   NO
    3. Can you change clothes in the dark?   YES   NO
    4 .Do you understand the terms "clean the dressing rooms" and "strike the set"?   YES   NO
    5. Do you know how to plunge a toilet?   YES   NO
    6. Would you be willing to have the cast party at your house?
                                                    YES   NO

Aunt Peg

Monday, December 3rd

Dear Aunt Peg:

Well, I just came back from auditioning for another play. You know how I always get the urge to do a play this time of year to get through the winter. The show is *Crossing Delancey* and there are parts for three women—a Jewish grandmother with arthritis, an overweight Jewish matchmaker, and a granddaughter in her late 20's/ early 30's. I'm too old for the part of Izzy (the granddaughter), but the role is so well written and tempting that I decided to give it a shot. I spent the afternoon pulling my grey hairs and trying to dress like I thought a young Jewish career woman would dress. I knew I was in trouble when I got to the theatre and found 15 actresses there all the right age.

The stage manager was handing out scripts to the young ladies and checking to make sure they were auditioning for the part of Izzy. When he got to me, he stopped and asked what part I was auditioning for. It should have been obvious! The problem may have been the way I was standing. I'd pulled my hair back with a rubber band and pinned on a big, bushy hairpiece thinking that it would make me look younger. Well, the rubber band made it look like I'd had a face lift (which was good), but the hairpiece was so heavy that I had to lean forward in order not to fall over backwards. I'm sure the stage manager thought I was auditioning for the part of the grandmother with arthritis.

The auditions were closed, which means we all had to wait in the lobby until we were called into the theatre to read from the script. There was nothing to do but sit there and size up the competition. I heard the gal next to me tell someone she'd spent the day trying to look older. I leaned over and told her that I had, too. She gave me a weird look.

Connie, a good friend of mine, came in to audition for the part of the matchmaker. We started exchanging stories about our most traumatic auditions and the horrible things directors had made us do—like pantomime or ad lib. We laughed about how we'd made complete fools out of ourselves and that we hoped this director wouldn't make us do anything like that. The next thing we knew, the girl sitting next to us packed up her things and left! Connie and I realized this would be a great way to cut down on our competition, so we continued telling stories (but weren't able to scare anybody else off).

I think I had a decent audition. Will just have to wait and see what the director wants. If he wants the oldest actress ever to play the part of Izzy, I've got the part.

Well, that's what's going on here. Please write—I love hearing from you.

Love,
Sally

Wednesday, December 5th

Dear Aunt Peg:

Guess what? I got the part!

Sally

Wednesday, January 2nd

Dear Aunt Peg:

Well, we had our first read-through last night. There are five characters in the play. Edith, the lady who plays my grandmother, seems a little scatterbrained, but that could work well for her character. I hope she enjoys learning lines. She's got a lot of them. My part is easy—all I have to do is sit and listen to her tell me stories.

I have two leading men—one who I have a crush on who I do a love scene with, and another who has a crush on me who I do a love scene with. Wonder how I'm going to like kissing two guys every night. Ha! The gal who plays the matchmaker is a lot of fun. Everyone is excited about getting started.

Oh—we have a vocal coach for this play. I've never had a vocal coach. Four of us are supposed to have Jewish accents of varying degrees—a strong one for grandma to a very slight one for Izzy. The vocal coach mentioned that this cold weather isn't good for our voices, so she told us to put a pan of water on our hot air registers at night for more humidity. I guess it won't hurt to try it.

What's the weather like in Ohio? Do you still take your walk every day? Say "hi" to your bridge group for me.

Love,

Sally

Wednesday, January 9th

Dear Aunt Peg:

Well, the vocal water didn't work. Remember I told you the vocal coach told us to put a pan of water on the hot air registers in our bedrooms at night? The cats drank it. They thought it was theirs. In fact, they've asked me to move their litter box into the bedroom as well so they won't have to go down to the basement. If I don't have a good voice for this show, I can blame it on them.

Rehearsals are going well. My part is a little bigger than I thought at first. Am spending all my free time trying to learn my lines. We blocked one of the kissing scenes last night. Jake is 12 inches (count 'em) taller than I am, and the director wants us to stand for the kiss. So Jake leans over as far as he can, and I get up on my toes and stretch as far as I can, but I can't in my wildest imagination believe that it's going to look very romantic. Oh, well.

Sorry to hear you have shingles. What are shingles?

Love,

Sally

Tuesday, January 22nd

Dear Aunt Peg:

Well, if I said I'd rather jump from an airplane (with my fear of heights) rather than do this play, would that give you the picture? For starters, my vocal coach says I'm not breathing properly. And if you don't breathe properly, you strain your vocal cords and lose your voice like I did last night. How could I not be breathing right? I've been breathing my whole life. Anyway, the fact that I don't know how to breathe is one of the better things that's happening with the play.

Edith, the woman who plays my grandmother, is driving me crazy. At rehearsals, I'll say a line and she'll stop and turn to the director and say: "Do you think I should be looking at Izzy during her line, or should I be ironing?" And the director will stop and tell her what she should be doing. Then I'll say my next line and Edith will stop and turn to the director and say: "Is my skirt going to have pockets? Because I'd like to be able to put my hands in my pockets." The director will stop and discuss costumes with her, knowing that if she doesn't, Edith will never move on. That's how the whole rehearsal goes.

We're supposed to have our lines memorized by now—little good that will do me since I'm going to run out of air in the middle of the play anyway—and this lady doesn't have a clue as to what her lines are. Since we're off-book, she just comes out onstage and ad libs. "This is where I give that speech about my brother Nathan, right? It's something about Mama, right?" And she'll turn to the stage manager and wait for him to read her lines.

She knows some of her lines, but she never says them in the same order, so I have no idea when to say my lines. Sometimes she'll say the key word at the beginning of her speech. Sometimes when I'm in the middle of my line, she'll remember more of her speech (that came before my line), and she'll interrupt me to finish her lines. It's awful! I've never worked with anyone like this. It means I'm going to have to learn her lines as well as mine so I'll know where we are in the play.

Then there's my costume. At the end of Act II, I'm supposed to come out in a "stunning" dress. That's what the playwright's directions say—a "stunning" dress. The costumer came rushing in last night and told the director she could only stay for 10 minutes. She brought the ugliest dress I've ever seen. It has a low-cut front—the girl it was made for had quite a bosom, which I don't have, so there's all this material just hanging there in front. You can see all the way down to my waist. The costumer asked me if I had a push-up bra. What does she think I'm going to push up?

The sleeves of the dress are about three inches longer than my arms, and the shoulders of the dress keep falling off my shoulders, but the costumer didn't think that would be a problem. Huh? Now, for the material. It's black velvet. The play takes place in summer, right? Plus the hips and legs are so tight I don't think I can barely walk in it, let alone step up onto an eight inch riser. The worst thing is, I have a half-page monologue about what a gorgeous dress I think this is, and how excited I am to be wearing it. I can see myself giving those lines while I'm hiking the shoulders of the dress back up onto my shoulders. Wish me luck.

We open next week. I told my friend Connie that the play was going badly and she said that even Charlton Heston made some movies that he knew weren't so good.

Bet he never had to wear an ugly dress.

Love,

Sally

Monday, February 11th

Dear Aunt Peg:

I loved your last letter! You always send me love and encouragement when I need it. No, I'll bet your neighbors don't think you're "touched" when you go out and walk in the rain. They probably wish they had the energy to go with you.

Well, somehow we got through opening night. Edith still doesn't know her lines. At one point during a blackout between scenes when Jake and I were heading backstage, Edith started to follow. Jake turned to her and said: "Edith, you don't exit. You're in this next scene." And Edith said: "I am?" And Jake said: "Yes, it's the sewing scene." And Edith said: "It is? I thought the sewing scene was in Act II." And Jake said: "This is Act II." I'm beginning to think she has Alzheimer's.

Remember I told you I have this big, romantic scene with Tyler? He comes dashing onstage, looks me in the eye, and says in a deep, booming voice: "Come, you must let me buy you a drink." Only last night he came bounding out onstage and got his tongue wrapped around his teeth and mistakenly said: "Come, you must let me buy you a dwink." It was so funny! I wanted to correct him and say: "Do you mean drink?" But I pretended that he said the right thing and went on. Actually, those are the moments that make the whole thing worthwhile. You test yourself. Can I say my next line without bursting into hysterical laughter like I'd like to?

The reviewers from the two local papers were there tonight. I think the show went pretty well. Wonder what they'll write. I'm glad you're feeling better. Shingles don't sound like fun at all.

Love,
Sally

Tuesday, February 19th
Dear Aunt Peg:
I'm enclosing copies of our two reviews. As you can see, one of

the reviewers loved the show except for me, and the other one loved me and hated the show. This was my first bad review. I'm handling it quite well. Every night before I go to bed I write the reviewer a letter. I say things like: "Dear Judith: Please tell me when you're going to play the part of Izzy. I want to come and see how to do it correctly." I don't send them, but writing them makes me feel better. Actually, her comment that I played the part like a "love-struck teenager" was a compliment. Remember how worried I was that I was too old for the part?

Six more shows. I can do it. I can do it. I can do it.

Bet you're excited about your trip to California. When do you leave?

Love,
Sally

Monday, February 25th
Dear Aunt Peg:
Well, it's finally over. I had all sorts of interesting things happen during the run of this play. I did one show with a twitch in my eye. I did another with hemorrhoids. I did several shows with the feeling that a big gorilla had his hands around my throat and was cutting the air off between my nose and my chest.

The worst thing that happened, though, was when I got something in my left contact lens during my big love scene with Jake. He was telling me how much he loved me. Tears were streaming down my face, and he thought it was because I was so moved by the scene. I was in pain. I kept hoping he'd hurry up so I could get offstage and clean my contacts. Anyway, he thought the scene was going so well that he became even more tender and slowed his lines way down. Finally, he realized that I was in misery, not love, and he finished his lines so we could get offstage.

For the last three shows, I took a new approach to acting with Edith. I decided that whenever she said (or did) something wrong, that I'd laugh. The stage manager came up to me during strike and told me I really looked like I was having a great time. Little did he know.

Why do I put myself through all this? Well, it's worth it to hear the audiences respond. Laughter is the best sound. Complete silence where there should have been laughter is the worst. Sometimes the audiences respond in ways you don't want them to. During one Sunday matinee, a lady in the front row turned to her friend and said: "I don't see how she thinks she's ever going to catch a man wearing THOSE shoes." In another scene, Jake asks me three questions and I answer "Yeah" to each one. Well, a lady in the audience figured out after my first "yeah" that I was going to say it again, so she proceeded to give my line for me the second two times. It was a little disconcerting. Should you even bother saying the line since it's already been said?

So, what did I learn from this experience? Two things. Kissing two guys every night is really quite pleasant. And second, if I ever see Edith at another audition I'm going to run the other way.

Love ya, Aunt Peg. Always did. Always will.

Sally

Does the Show Have to Go On?

Acting in plays is my favorite thing in the world. But it's time-consuming and stressful. It really throws my life off. I usually spend about a month at rehearsals, a month doing the show, and a month recovering.

To accommodate my love of performing, yet keep my stress to a manageable level, I assembled a group of actor-friends and created a group called the Civic Theatre Comedy Readers. We read jokes and humorous stories as entertainment to audiences around town. This form of "reader's theatre" is wonderfully simple. It doesn't require any memorization of lines, any rehearsals, any costumes, or any sets. We just stand in front of an audience and read.

It's always been our dream to read for a really large audience. Recently we had the chance. Every year, as a fund-raising event, our local hospital sponsors a summer fair at the fairgrounds. When the coordinator of that event called to invite the Comedy Readers to read on the "main stage" at the fairgrounds coliseum, I jumped at the chance and quickly said "Yes!" We'd never performed on a "main stage" before. This could be our ticket to stardom! When I told the comedy readers the news, we all had visions of happy fairgoers, tilt-a-wheels, and our names in flashing lights over the coliseum door.

My niece Katie agreed to perform with us, so on the day of our performance, I picked her up at her dorm.

"I haven't seen the Comedy Readers advertised anywhere," she said as she pulled the car door shut.

"Not to worry," I said. "It's at the fairgrounds. There's going to be a big crowd."

"Why are you wearing white tennis shoes?" she asked. "I was at the fair yesterday and it was muddy."

"Not to worry," I said. "We're going to be inside on the "main stage.""

Unfortunately, no one had heard of us at the performers' entrance, so we ended up having to park in the main parking lot and lug six music stands through the mud to the main building. There went my new white tennis shoes. When we entered the building, Katie and I stopped and stared. I don't know what I thought a coliseum would be like, but this was a barn. It had bleachers on the sides, a stage at the far end, and rows of folding chairs on a dirt floor.

"It's going to be fine," I said weakly.

When the other readers arrived, they didn't seem any more enthusiastic about our venue than Katie did. They also noticed there was no audience. "Has this been advertised?" they asked. "We're in the program," Doc said. "That's us," he said, pointing to a teeny square with teeny print on the printed schedule he picked up at the entrance.

Meanwhile, up onstage, a nurse was describing the different features of baby seats to an audience of five. She finished promptly at 1:00 p.m. and departed, along with the audience. The cast and I looked at each other. The barn was completely empty. "Well, let's go on!" I said cheerfully. We walked slowly up the steps to the stage and stood there. Chris noticed a few folding chairs in the wings, so we set them out and sat and waited for our audience.

"Maybe if we start, people will come," Doc suggested after a long, quiet spell.

I went to the microphone, introduced myself, and said how thrilled we were to be there. Then I introduced the members of the cast, who each glared at me, unhappy about having given up their Saturday afternoon. Half-way through the introductions, a lady came up to the foot of the stage and interrupted . "Excuse me, is this where the baby judging contest is going to be?"

Doc looked at his printed schedule of events and told her that "yes," the baby judging contest would start in a half hour. Off she went. Doc yelled: "You're welcome to stay!" but we saw her heading to the corn dog stand. We were obviously no competition with corn dogs.

After naming the members of the cast, I introduced Richard, the managing director of Civic Theatre, and asked him to give a plug for *Brigadoon*, the show that Civic Theatre was currently doing. Richard stood up, went to the microphone, and said: "We're all sold out," and sat back down. I was hoping he could have killed a little more time than that. I must admit, it was disconcerting to talk to a huge, empty barn.

We started our program, and lo and behold, people did start to trickle in. Most of them were mothers with young children and babies (in strollers) who were obviously going to be in the baby contest. The mothers were all brushing their kids' hair and changing their babies' diapers. No one looked up at us to acknowledge our presence. It's like we were invisible.

The acoustics in the barn were so poor, we couldn't hear each other read, even though we were right there with them on the stage. Because of that, we couldn't give each other encouragement or laugh at each other's jokes. We had no idea how things were going. There was one lady who looked like she was laughing, but she was so far away we couldn't hear her. If she was laughing, there was a good chance she was laughing at us.

As Murphy said, things can always get worse. And they did. Because of the influx of people for the baby show, there was a lot more noise. On their way in, all the little kids had been given wooden noisemakers which they were using to hit each other over the head with. One little boy was running up and down on the bleachers to see how much noise he could make. Another little boy was kicking the dirt in front of the stage and sending up great clouds of dust. About half-way back in the audience, a baby started to cry, and all the others followed suit. And if that wasn't bad enough, a fife and drum corps—complete with a bagpipe and troop of drummers— began playing right outside the entrance.

By this time, the cast was really surly. Whenever it was time for one of them to read, they'd look at me and mouth: "Do I have to?" I'd nod and point to the microphone.

We had just one more piece to read to complete our program when I felt a tap on my shoulder. I twisted around and saw the organizer of the event crouched behind my folding chair. Her question topped off my day.

She said: "Do you mind getting off? We need the stage."

The Sardine and Onion Sandwich

What I like best about acting is that it's mentally, physically, and emotionally challenging. Most of the time I bumble my way through life, but when I'm in a play I have to stay focused and precise. And that's good for me.

One way I stay focused is by sticking to my rule to never date my leading men. (At least not until the play is over.) The reason is simple: if the romantic relationship were to go south, I'd be stuck with an awkward—or miserable—relationship onstage. By the time I reach the end of a play, I'm sick of everyone anyway, so this has never been an issue.

But then there's the story of Bob Barrett and the sardine and onion sandwich.

One winter, I was cast in the part of the married daughter in a production of *Never Too Late*. Bob Barrett, a radio D.J. who was new to the area, was cast in the role of my husband.

Both Bob and I were single and we started going out to grab a bite to eat after rehearsals. Every night, when we got to "our" pub, Bob would excuse himself and call in to his radio station to make sure everything was all right. He explained that he had the kind of job where he could be called back to work at a moment's notice to solve a problem or fill in for a fellow D.J.

It soon became obvious that Bob wanted our relationship to be more than just friends. After dinner one night, he tried to kiss me. I pulled back, explaining my rule to never, ever date anyone I was in a play with until the show was over.

That winter was the worst winter of the decade. Record snowfalls. Blizzard after blizzard. Mounds of snow everywhere. Lafayette looked like Siberia—except without the wolves. Now, Bob lived about 30 miles away. One evening the blizzard became so bad during our rehearsal that, unbeknownst to us, the state police closed all the roads. Realizing that Bob would never make it home, I offered to let him come home with me and sleep on my couch. As usual, Bob called the radio station to let them know where he was. Then he followed me to my apartment (with a snow plow escort), and spent the night. This went on for about a week, with Bob sleeping on my couch.

Eventually the weather improved and Bob was able to start commuting back home again. Before he packed up his things, he told me he was falling in love with me. He even mentioned the word "marriage." Now, I was really enjoying being in the play, and didn't want anything to screw that up, so I held firm to my rule about not getting involved with him until after the play was over.

Since I had several really quick changes in the play, they assigned me a dresser. Rhoda was a God-send. When I'd exit the stage, I'd let the costume I was wearing fall to the floor while Rhoda pulled my next costume on over my head. And I'd go rushing back out onstage. Obviously, Rhoda got to see me a lot in my underwear.

And because of that (or maybe despite that), Rhoda and I quickly became friends.

Opening night arrived. The play went exceedingly well. After the show, I looked around for Bob. I couldn't find him. That was strange. So I went to the cast party with Rhoda. I was surprised Bob hadn't offered to escort me to the party. But not as surprised as I was when he walked in with the young gal who was running the lights for the show.

Huh? What was that all about? I pulled Rhoda into the nearest bedroom and asked her if she knew how infatuated Bob was with me. She stared at me blankly.

I told her he'd even mentioned "marriage."

Another blank look.

Then she confessed: "Well, he's spent every night this past week on my couch."

What? He'd told me he was going home! And now he was necking with the lighting gal?

The next evening when I arrived at the theatre, Bob met me at my car and handed me a large, oversized Valentine card. (It was Valentine's Day.) During intermission, I showed it to Rhoda. She reached into her bag and brought out the card Bob had given her. They were identical. We went over to the lighting gal (Bob had dumped her and was in the wings flirting with the stage manager) and asked her if Bob had given her anything for Valentine's Day. She pulled out a third, identical card.

That did it. This guy needed to learn a lesson.

That night, the three of us bought some wine in a box and went to Rhoda's apartment to brainstorm ways to embarrass him—

preferably in public. One idea was to throw a cream pie in his face during curtain call. That didn't seem to be payback enough. As we finished the box of wine, we came up with it.

We'd make him a sardine and onion sandwich.

You see, there's a scene in the play where Bob's character has to eat a sardine and onion sandwich. I mean, he has to eat the entire sandwich. During "tech" week, the property mistress asked him what foods he liked, and every night she'd make him a fresh, modest sandwich that he could swallow easily while saying his lines.

Rhoda and I decided that for the final performance, we would make his sandwich. We sneaked in bread, an onion, and a can of sardines. Minutes before I was to take the sandwich onstage, Rhoda and I locked ourselves in the dressing room and prepared our treat. We laid four fat, juicy sardines—with their tails sticking out—on a slice of bread, then added a thick slice of onion. We topped it off with another slice of bread. Unlocking the door and looking around to make sure nobody had seen us, I carried the plate with the sandwich backstage to where I was to make my entrance.

Seconds before I was to go on, the property mistress (holding the legitimate sandwich) saw me holding mine. She knew something was up.

"You can't use that!" she whispered. I smiled wickedly.

She grabbed my plate and tried to get it away from me. I pulled it back. She pulled it her way. I pulled it back. Then I heard my cue to go out onstage. Finally, with one last great effort, I got the plate away from her and bounded out onstage.

When Bob saw the sandwich, he got a sick look on his face. I had the joy of watching him—with childlike innocence—as he chewed and swallowed each bite. I'm sure he was trying to figure out who was responsible for the sandwich. It could have been so many of us.

After the show, he raced out of the theatre (still in makeup and costume) and drove off, never to be seen again.

But that's not the end of the story.

A month after the show closed, the local university asked us to perform the production on their main stage for a large convention of homemakers. That night, Bob brought a woman along with him and seated her carefully on a chair in the wings—right behind the curtain where we made our entrances and exits. We kept tripping over her every time we had an entrance or an exit. We figured he'd brought her to guard the sandwich.

We were all dying to know who she was.

The property mistress (who still felt sorry for Bob for the prank we pulled on him) decided to go over and ask her.

"Oh," she said. "I'm Bob's wife."

Surviving in the Wilderness

I'm a great believer in learning new things, so whenever possible, I take classes at night, after I get off work. I've taken everything from basic auto mechanics to natural childbirth classes, an interesting choice since I've never had any kids (except for the baby I had with Cassey). This fall, as I was leafing through the list of courses being offered, I came across one entitled: "How to Survive the Unexpected."

Now, to me, a course like that would include such things as what to do when you invite your boss and his wife over for dinner and she announces she hates eggs (and you've made quiche). Or, what to do if your guy invites you to spend the weekend with him when he has his kids, and the kids make it perfectly clear (when he's not around) that they don't like you. In any event, I figured there'd be something in the course I could use, so I enrolled.

My first clue the class was going to be different was that it met in the Armory instead of in a regular classroom. My second clue came when I walked into class the first night and saw everyone dressed in down-filled vests, flannel shirts, and hiking boots. I was wearing a suit. They'd all walked or bicycled to class. I'd parked as close to the building as I could. They carried their books in well-worn rucksacks. I had a leather briefcase, which I tucked under my seat as far as I could.

According to the instructor, we were going to be covering such things as arctic survival, desert survival, jungle survival, survival at sea, and how to survive in the wilderness. We'd learn how to find food and water, how to build a fire, how to exit a submerged vehicle, and how to fight off an attack by a wild animal. Considering some of the men I've been out with, that technique could come in useful.

As the instructor described the course, I wondered if I'd made a mistake. I am not an outdoors person. When the instructor asked us to go around the room and give our experience in the outdoors, I slid down in my seat. My only experience was the summer my parents took our family camping. I stayed in the car and read novels while everybody else went out looking for rocks. (No kidding—my family was into rock-hunting.) In the evenings, I'd make a mad dash from the car to the tent—and that was the extent of my experience in the outdoors.

The rest of the class had backpacked, white water rafted, spelunked, catamaraned, and rappelled. As it turned out, the most experienced person in the class was the other female in the group—a delightful English woman with a fine British accent who had climbed the Matterhorn.

By some stroke of luck, the instructor forgot to call on me. I made a note to try to do some "outdoors thing" by the next class meeting so I'd have something to say.

I enjoy talking in class, and soon had my first chance. The instructor posed a hypothetical situation:

"Your plane has just crashed in the mountains. What is the first thing you need?"

I knew the answer was "water," but decided to play it cool and let someone else answer.

"A will to live," Jamie said.

What a dumb thing to say! I smiled smugly and waited for the instructor to correct him.

"That's right—a will to live," said the instructor.

I erased "water" in my notes and wrote "a will to live." For the rest of the evening, I kept my mouth shut.

The lecture that night was on how to predict the weather. According to the instructor, people often get caught in crisis situations they could have prevented if they'd done a little amateur weather forecasting. He explained the difference between "high" and "low" pressure systems. He told us various sayings that have been passed down through the years, like "red sky at night, sailors delight," and "red sky in the morning, sailors take warning." He also told us to check our canoes in the morning. If you wake up and your canoe has dew on it, it probably won't rain that day. And conversely, if your canoe is not covered with dew, the chances are good that it will rain.

Now, I don't camp. I don't boat. And I hate getting up early. The thought of me waking up to check the dew on my canoe was so funny that I threw my head back and started laughing. As I looked around the room to see who else was laughing, I saw everyone diligently writing the information down. So I wrote it down, too.

Of all the topics in the course, the one that hit closest to home was the session on cold-weather survival. The instructor taught us how to pack a survival kit to keep in our cars. He warned us against wearing cotton next to our skin because when cotton gets wet, it conducts heat away from the body. And, he said, if we were ever in a situation where we found ourselves shivering uncontrollably, we should build a fire to get warm. If we were with someone who was shivering uncontrollably, we should get them to shelter, give them something warm to drink, remove their clothing, and apply external heat. (In other words, someone needs to crawl into the sleeping bag with them.) When the instructor added that research showed recovery would be hastened if the second person was a member of the opposite sex, the guy sitting next to me leaned over, smiled, and asked if I was cold.

I smiled back. In your dreams.

Even though I couldn't see myself climbing the Matterhorn or trekking to the Arctic, the topics we studied did make for great dinner conversation. Like, you shouldn't drink water from a lake that has dead animals around it. Animal dung burns well. Porcupines taste better if you club them over the head rather than shoot them. But, as interesting as the class was, I still hadn't found anything I could use.

Until we got to the lecture on hotel fires. Now we were talking my language. The instructor told us that the safest place to stay in a hotel was on the first or second floor because then, if you had to jump, you could. That night in class, I decided that from then on, I'd stay in a room on the first or second floor.

I didn't have long to wait. That weekend, I was headed to a conference in Miami Beach. All through the flight, I reviewed my class notes. I was excited that I might actually have a chance to use my survival techniques!

When I arrived at the hotel, I checked in at the front desk.

The manager told me he was holding a lovely room for me on their newly-decorated ninth floor.

"I'm sorry," I said. "I need a room on the first floor."

He explained that the room he was holding for me was one of their best rooms.

I said that was nice, but that I wanted a room on the first floor.

He looked in his computer and frowned. "How strongly do you feel about that?"

I remained adamant. "It must be on the first floor."

He reluctantly handed me a key and directed me to the rear of the hotel. I picked up my bags, exited through the double glass doors at the rear of the lobby, and found myself standing in the sand, just a few yards away from the water. It was dark. There were no lights. I inched my way along the wall until I reached room #1. I opened the door, set my bags down, and looked around. The bed wasn't made, the paint was peeling from the walls, and half the lamps didn't have light bulbs. But the most glaring omission was that the door had no lock.

I could envision all sorts of sleazy characters coming in and out of the room all night. Don't get me wrong. I like men. It's just that I prefer to choose my own. We hadn't covered "be sure to get a room with a door that locks" in our survival class, but common sense told me I'd sleep better if I could lock the door. So I slung my bags over my shoulder and schlepped across the beach again, trekking sand back through the lobby to the front desk. The beautiful room on the ninth floor didn't sound nearly so bad.

At the front desk, I told the manager I'd changed my mind— I'd decided to take the room on the ninth floor. He informed me he'd just given it away.

Of course.

He did have a room on the third floor, which I took. I figured that would be a good compromise between being burgled on the first floor and breaking my legs if I had to jump from the ninth floor. I slept soundly that night, knowing that now I had an experience "in the wilderness" to talk about at our next class.

I would encourage everyone to take a course like this. Not only will it give you lots of good stories to tell, but it just might save your life.

Look at me. My confidence has really increased. I'm sure now that I could survive any unexpected situation.

As long as I have my class notes with me.

Exercise Videos

$\mathcal{A}$s I was making a mad dash into the ladies room the other day, I happened to catch a glimpse of myself in a full-length mirror. When I backed up to take a second look, a little voice in the back of my head asked:

a) Are those really our hips?
b) Didn't we used to be thin? and,
c) How long have we been wearing skirts with elastic waistbands?

It was a humbling experience. I suddenly realized I'd been avoiding full-length mirrors . . . and why. Confronting my image head-on, I decided to make the classic New Year's resolution. I decided to lose weight. Even if it meant—gulp—having to exercise.

That evening I went over to Susie's house. Susie had a great figure.

"How do you keep in shape?" I asked.

"Exercise DVDs," she replied.

"Exercise DVDs?"

"Want to borrow one?" She went to her bookcase, pulled a DVD off the shelf and handed it to me. "I guarantee—this will work." She had to be kidding. How could watching a DVD help?

Skeptically, I took the DVD home and read the accompanying literature. According to the brochure, I was going to use weights to build up the upper part of my body, and a step-up box to trim my legs, hips, and thighs. I was encouraged to purchase the company's special weights and step-up boxes, along with their personal brand of exercise attire. To assist me in making these purchases, they provided a toll free number. And while I was at it—if I wanted to get the maximum benefit from the program—they suggested I purchase the seven additional tapes in the series. By using different tapes when I exercised, I would achieve "muscle confusion." And that (somehow) was going to help my legs get thinner.

"Yeah, right," my cynic sneered.

As long as I had the DVD, I figured I'd give it a try. So, minus the official weights, leotards, and step-up box, I cleared a place in my living room, inserted the DVD into my DVD player, and hit "play."

The first thing I noticed was the instructor. She was beautiful—lean, with long, blonde hair and a perfect complexion. And she was cheerful. "She can't be real," I thought, standing there in my baggy sweat suit. "She must be computer-generated." I was so engrossed in watching her move—like a ballerina—that I forgot to follow along. When I came back to reality and tried to bend over like she was doing, I discovered I could only reach my knees. The instructor, on the other hand, was touching her palms flat on the floor.

"So I need a little work," I thought. "Pretty soon I'll be touching the floor, too."

"Yeah, right," my cynic sneered.

As the instructor began jogging in place, the camera panned the class. There were about 20 students, all beautiful and lean, with long, blonde hair and perfect complexions. And they were cheerful. "I knew it!" I shouted to my cats. "Nobody looks like that! They're computer-generated."

After watching the DVD all the way through, I started it again and attempted some of the moves. Much to my surprise, it was fairly enjoyable. The instructor was encouraging, the music was up-beat, and there were lots of dance movements, which I liked. I actually made it through to the end of the DVD.

Every night that week I came home from work and exercised to the DVD. In fact, I found myself looking forward to coming home and exercising. It was certainly the highlight of my cats' day. My eight-pound Siamese cat, Miss Suey, batted my legs when I was doing jumping jacks. My 12- pound Siamese, Heathcliff, sat on my chest and kneaded my neck while I was doing crunches. I figured that in many ways, I was in even better shape than the instructor. I never saw her exercising with cats.

After about a week, I decided I was ready to try some weights, so I bought some little pink barbells. After about two weeks, I decided I was ready for a step-up box. Not wanting to fork over money for the official version, I did the next best thing—I turned my blue, plastic kitchen dishpan upside down.

Except for the fact that it made an odd sort of "smooshing" noise every time I stepped on and off, it worked quite well. But several minutes into the tape, the dishpan began to sag in the middle and my feet turned precariously inward. When I stepped up with my right foot, I leaned to the left. When I stepped up with my left foot,

I leaned to the right. So I went to the basement, found a board, and laid it on top of the dishpan. Aha! I was able to stairstep in earnest, just like they were on the tape. It may have looked silly, but I was exercising.

I enjoyed that DVD so much, I returned it to Susie and sent away for the next two DVDs. The program was right—by trading off and doing different tapes, you didn't get bored.

I was working my way through the seven tapes, and everything was going fine until tape #8. Tape #8 was advertised as the "best, the newest, and the toughest" of all the tapes. And it was. In tape #8 there was no beautiful ballerina; the instructor was a huge, German Brunhilda sort of creature with bulging muscles . . . who didn't smile. She used a large barbell with hundreds of pounds of weights. And she sweated! The ballerinas never sweated!

When the camera panned the class, I noticed there were only three students. They could only find three people who could do these exercises! And nobody looked happy. I gave myself a pep-talk. If I could master the seven other tapes, I could master this one. I went to my kitchen closet, got out my barbell (aka broom), and began to follow along.

No way. My DVD player didn't have a "half-speed" setting. I ended up just sitting there, in amazement, hoping I could get something out of the tape by just watching it. I gave up. There was no way I was going to be able to do this tape. Tape #8 is going to make a great present if I ever want to get back at someone.

In any event, I'm now a firm believer in exercise DVDs. I like being able to exercise when I want to, and in the privacy of my own living room. I especially like how my figure has improved. Yesterday

I bought a skirt with a real waistband.

I don't know if all exercise videos are this good, but if you're interested in getting in shape, and you've never tried one before, you should try it. Then the next time you go into a ladies room, maybe you won't have to hurry so fast past that full-length mirror . . .

EVERYDAY PROBLEMS

Why Can't I Communicate?

I used to be able to communicate with people. Not just talk, but actually communicate. I understood what they meant, and they understood what I meant.

That doesn't happen any more. Has the world changed? Was I just delusional, thinking that I was communicating? Or, have I just gotten old? For instance, take this past week. Here are some of the things I've read (that I haven't understood), or people have said to me (that I haven't understood):

Replying to my offer of a ride to church, my friend responded: "I won't call you if I don't need a ride." Huh? (Actually, this is reminiscent of the instructions for figuring line 1 on Schedule 1 of your Indiana state income tax: "If you did not complete Federal Schedules C, C-EZ, E, or F, which include sole proprietorship income, farm income, rental, partnership, S corporation, and trust and estate income (or loss), then do not complete this line.) Huh?

In a pharmacy lecture on the topic of diabetes that I was observing, the instructor kept referring to "non sugar-free food." Hearing that gave me a headache. I kept thinking: wouldn't "non sugar-free food" have sugar in it? Wouldn't it have been easier for him to have referred to it as "food that has sugar in it?"

I bought a pair of winter socks. The tag read "Do not iron." Were they serious? Who irons their socks?

I ordered a bra advertised in the newspaper for $7.95. When it arrived, there was a note enclosed that read: "Be sure to use the delicate cycle when washing and drying all fine lingerie." Who calls a bra that cost $7.95 "fine lingerie"?

Truth be told, there are entire groups of people I have trouble communicating with. Like doctors. Yesterday, the doctor at Urgent Care told me my rash wouldn't spread. He had to be nuts. Rashes always spread. The pharmacist who then gave me the medicine for my rash assured me that it wouldn't taste bad and that it wouldn't make me drowsy. Who was she kidding? All medicines taste bad. All medicines that aren't supposed to make you drowsy make you drowsy.

Then there's my dentist. Before he drills, he says: "Tell me if this hurts." My thought is: Well, don't do anything that will make it hurt. Or, he'll say: "Is this Okay?" Okay compared to what? He's pounding on my tooth with a hammer. How can that possibly be Okay? He also likes to tell me to relax my tongue. Nobody ever taught me how to relax my tongue. How many other life skills like that am I missing?

Repairmen are another group of people I have trouble communicating with. When I needed my refrigerator serviced, "Joe" came in, set his toolbox down, looked at the refrigerator and said: "Gee, I've never seen one of these before." That comment did not instill in me a great deal of confidence in him. "Joe" had a "brother" who was a furnace repairman. When my furnace konked out, "Jim" came in, set his tools down, looked at my furnace and said (dumbfoundedly): "Huh. I've never seen one of these before." Wonderful. Those two guys had a third brother who was a plumber. The plumber hauled armloads of equipment into the basement to unclog my sewer line, then said (taking his cap off and scratching his head): "Gee, I've never seen a set-up like this before."

Great. I'm so glad I can help you guys learn your trade.

But the group of people I have the most trouble communicating with is my students. My students say things that either: (1) make no sense, or (2) have nothing to do with what's being discussed. For example, after failing an exam, a student once screamed: "My psychiatrist told me I'm ready to be back with people again!" How should I have responded to that?

Another student, upset about earning a "C" in the course, followed me down the hallway yelling: "I took this course for an easy 'A'!" I can't imagine telling my class it would be an easy "A." Do you suppose I did and just forgot?

One of my all-time favorite lines came when I was collecting a homework assignment. John, explaining why he didn't have his homework, said: "My homework didn't come with me." Huh? Since when does homework have a mind of its own? Did his homework wake up that morning and suddenly decide it didn't want to go to class?

Then there's my boss. On my latest performance review, my boss said: "You're doing a great job, but I'd like to see more stress in your job." Huh? You mean I shouldn't work ahead and finish my projects before they're due? Or, I shouldn't solve crises myself? I should bring them to you? Maybe she just wants me to look more stressed. If it would help me get a raise, I'd be happy to start looking more drained at the end of the day.

Then there's my hair. I don't know the right words to get my hair done.

Stylist: "What are we going to do today?

Me: "Well, I want this piece of hair to go up . . . and . . . this piece of hair to go down . . . and this piece to go . . . more over there."

Stylist: "So, you want the back layered?"

What the hell is "layered"? Was that something I was supposed to learn back in the fourth grade? I may have had the measles then.

My mother was the first person who tried to mess up my mind. Every Christmas Eve when she'd tuck me in, she'd tell me to "sleep fast." I'd lie awake all night trying to figure how to do that. To this day, it bothers me I don't know how.

I remember my parents shaking their heads a lot when I was growing up. Now I know why. These days, I find myself shaking my head a lot, too. It's a rare treat for me to get through a day without encountering someone I don't have trouble communicating with. It's rarer still to have someone who's talking to me say: "I know exactly what you mean."

I've decided that from now on, whenever I have trouble making myself understood, I'm going to just keep talking until the other guy shakes his head. I even have a strategy so that people at fast food restaurants won't ask me if I want "fries with that" (when I haven't asked for them). The next time I pull up to a drive-through window, I'm going to say:

"Listen very carefully. I don't want fries. I just want a coke."

They'll still ask.

Stuck in an Elevator

I work on the seventh floor. I could take the stairs, but that's not nearly as exciting as visiting with people on an elevator. No, wait. People don't talk to each other on elevators. I'm thinking about something else. Anyway, yesterday when I left work, I called the elevator (as usual), stepped in when it arrived (as usual) and watched as the doors closed (as usual). I pressed "M" for main floor. The elevator descended to the sixth floor, and instead of the doors opening for someone to get on, the elevator car sat there and just shook up and down. From somewhere in the ceiling a recording came on which said: "We're experiencing minor technical difficulties."

Well, now that was a new experience. "Minor technical difficulties." Several questions came to my mind. What would "minor technical difficulties" be? Could "minor" difficulties lead to "major" technical difficulties? What would major difficulties be?

I knew nothing bad could happen to me (nobody dies in an elevator), so I stood there and assessed my situation. Did I have anything with me to eat? No. Did I have my cell phone? Nope. I must have left it in my office. I considered sitting down on the floor to wait, but it wasn't very clean. So I just stood there.

And waited.

And waited.

And waited some more.

Nothing happened.

Then, with a jerk, the elevator started up again. Good sign! It descended to the fifth floor and stopped. Then it shook. This time, it shook up and down . . . and side to side. Whoa! That was new. The recording came on again. "We're experiencing minor difficulties." Who is we, kimosabe?

I waited for about a minute and then decided what the hell, why don't I use the little emergency phone they provide. At least I could talk to someone while I was stuck. So I pushed the button that said: "phone."

Ring, ring. "Yes?"

"Hello there. Uh, I seem to be stuck in an elevator," I said as cheerfully as possible, making an attempt to establish rapport with the person at the other end of the line since I knew I could be in there for awhile.

"We'll send someone shortly." And he hung up on me. He hung up on me! You can't hang up on me! I'm stuck in an elevator! At the very least he should have introduced himself. Who was he? Where was he? When he said: "We'll send someone shortly," who was he talking about? An elevator repairman? A firefighter? A news team? Should I fluff up my hair? And where is this person coming from? Indianapolis? And how long is shortly? Shortly to whom? That guy, or me?

I figured he was probably just having a bad day, so I forgave him and continued waiting. Suddenly the elevator started up again. Yeah! It descended to the fourth floor, stopped, and shook. Up and down. Side to side. And this time it tilted upper left to lower right. The recording came on again. "We're experiencing minor difficulties." Even the recording sounded more panicked. I decided to use the phone again. Surely this time I'd get someone who would "talk me down" like they do when you're the only person on an airplane and the pilot has died and you have to land the plane.

Ring, ring. "Yes?" Now the elevator was shaking—in place. I tried to remain calm but I heard someone yell "Get me out of here!" and I think it was me. The guy said: "We'll send someone shortly." And he hung up on me. Again! I couldn't believe it! He was the same grumpy guy who answered the phone the first time! Or, wait. Maybe it wasn't a guy. Maybe it was a recording. Surely it wasn't a recording! If it was a recording, maybe nobody knew I was stuck in the elevator. It was Friday. After five. I could be in there all weekend!

The elevator continued its descent, floor by floor, stopping at each floor to rock and shake. Eventually it made it to the first floor. The little red light above the doors indicated that we were on "Main," but the doors didn't open. Obviously it wasn't going to help to call on the phone. So I thought, if I hit the "door open" button, what was the worst that would happen? I'd see a brick wall. I figured I could cope with that. So I pushed the "door open" button. Miraculously, the doors opened and I escaped.

Where did I go? Not home. I went looking for the guy who was on the other end of the elevator phone. We were going to have a little talk, starting with the definitions of the words: "minor," "we," and "shortly."

Footnote: I told this story to my friend Diane and she told me about the time she got stuck in an elevator in the parking garage across from her work in downtown Birmingham. If you get stuck in the elevator there and try to use the phone, it rings to a receiver mounted on the outside of the building. There's a small sign by the receiver that tells people who are passing, that if they hear the phone ringing, to go around the corner and report it to the parking garage office. Luckily, someone heard her ring, but Diane said after that she always took the stairs.

Me, too.

The Day from Hell

Once, when I was complaining about my day to my sister-in-law, she told me "not every day can be a good day." I was reminded of that yesterday when I had the day from hell. Actually, none of the things that happened was really bad. It's just that they all occurred on the same day.

Setting: Roughly 5:50 a.m. on a bitterly cold, dark, January morning.

I awoke, not to the sound of my alarm, but to the sound of my cat throwing up on my pillow.

Stripped the bed. Carried the blankets and sheets from my bedroom (on the second floor) to the washer and dryer (in the basement). Had to skip breakfast because I was running late.

Brushed the three inches of snow off my car. Scraped the ice off the windshield as best I could.

Decided to drive through McDonald's to get breakfast.

Started to get in a better mood even though everyone in the world was in the drive-through line.

Went to place my order when I discovered that my driver's window wouldn't roll down. (Frozen.) Had to open my door and yell my order at the little box.

Closed my door and pulled forward.

Stopped at the window where you pay, knowing that I was going to have to open my door again. Dilemma: how far should I pull past the window so I could open my door to hand the gal my money? Realized I'd pulled up too far. Was going to have to back up. Impossible. Everyone in line had pulled up directly behind me. Stuck my head out my door and waved my arm to get them all to back up.

Made it to work. My breakfast froze between the parking garage and my office.

Turned my computer on. Searched Google for a map of the United States for a tutoring session I had on Saturday. Got the map, along with a big red box that yelled "VIRUS" on my screen. Couldn't get rid of it.

Called the computer service repair guy who arrived two hours later.

Computer guy worked on computer and announced that it was fixed, but that he'd lost all of my emails.

Went for a coffee break.

Returned to the office, sat down at my desk, and turned my computer back on. The same big red VIRUS box appeared on the screen. Called the service repair guy. He said he'd send his boss over.

"Boss" came over—two hours later—and worked on my computer. He said he fixed it, but unfortunately had lost all of my Microsoft word documents.

Put my forehead down on my desk and cried.

Tried to cheer myself up by going to lunch. Discovered I didn't have my debit card and had to borrow money for lunch.

Returned from lunch (still 20 degrees outside, but now there was a wind). Only had one of my $30.00 Columbia gloves. The other one must have fallen out of my pocket. Did not want to go back out into the cold to find it. Would buy a new pair in the spring.

Told a friend I was going on a cruise to Mexico. She went on and on about how awful cruises were. (She'd never been on one herself.)

My secretary fixed my computer. (It took her about 10 minutes.) She was able to retrieve all of my emails and documents.

Did some work.

Found my lost glove on the seat of a chair here in the office as I was leaving to go home.

Got home and opened my mail. The new bra I'd ordered had arrived. Included in the package was a note from the company saying they were sorry but they were out of the item I'd ordered, so they were sending me a substitution and hoped that would be okay. I'd ordered a bra, size 38. They sent me a bra, size 44. I could see substituting on the basis of color, but not on the basis of size. Would now need to make a trip to the post office and send it back.

Searched the house for my debit card. Found it in the pocket of a coat I never wear.

Stretched out in my recliner, pulled a blanket over myself, and turned on the TV to watch *House MD*. This was the one good thing that was going to happen to me for the day. No show. I'd forgotten to turn my VCR on to record it.

Went to bed. Locked the cat out of the bedroom. Pulled the covers up over my head and prayed that tomorrow was going to be better.

Too Many Chairs in the Lab

I teach at a university. My colleagues and I were having coffee the other day when the topic of end-of-semester course/instructor evaluations came up. As we talked, we discovered that recently, we'd all received comments from students on our end-of-the-semester evaluations that didn't make sense. For example, one of my colleagues received a negative evaluation from a student who complained that "there were too many chairs in the lab." It wasn't clear to us how the number of chairs would affect learning or how a comment like that was going to help us improve our teaching. Was that student being funny, or was he serious?

The problem is, sometimes students make comments that aren't constructive. For instance, answers like "the time he told a joke" and "the time he used the board" to the question: "What did you like best about this course?" aren't particularly helpful.

So I asked my colleagues if I could review their evaluations to see if I could come up with some common themes. By looking at the evaluations as a group, maybe I could determine how we could better help our students learn. Here's what I came up with:

1. First and foremost, don't teach too much. Students rarely said they liked a course because it was academically challenging or that they learned a lot. In fact, students in one class reported what they liked best about their course was that "there was no pressure to learn." Either learning came easy for them (hence they didn't feel pressured into doing it), or else they didn't learn anything (which was all right with them).

2. Be careful where and when you hold your class. Students preferred classes that met in buildings close to their residence halls and towards the middle of the day. Seven-thirty was too early for a class; 4:30 too late. Students also felt that there should be no class on the 28th of February. (I have no idea why.)

3. Don't have a textbook. If a text is required, it should be lightweight and the chapters should be short.

4. Don't assign any homework. If homework is assigned, it should be minimal.

5. Don't have labs, quizzes, tests, or final exams.

6. Do have guest speakers. Preferably a large number, and preferably you won't hold them accountable for what the speakers said.

7. Have plenty of breaks.

8. Let the students out of class early.

9. Have a Christmas party.

10. Look good. Students liked male instructors who had "interesting ties" and female instructors who "looked nice."

11. Provide snacks of some sort—candy, cookies, cake, or donuts—on a regular basis. (Students especially like "real" cream for their coffee.)

Sometime students suggestions on how the instructor could

improve his/her course were quite specific. I was fascinated by the proposal "this content should be in another course." What was the problem with having it in that course? The suggestion: "need new book with the same content" also caught my attention. Wouldn't a different book with the same content be the same book?

Students in an English class had the following complaint: "The problem with the essays is that you have to think." Obviously, they would have preferred writing essays which didn't require any thinking. Creating assignments where students don't have to think could put English teachers in a bind—or out of work.

In regards to lectures, students in a Consumer Science class wanted their instructor to "gear the lectures specifically toward the material we'll be tested on, rather than seemingly frivolous material and trivial information from work experience." Obviously, this class would prefer that the instructor keep his work experience to himself. On the other hand, students in a management class probably would have liked to have heard about their instructor's work experience. They complained that their course had too many theories. And worse—that the theories overlapped. My heart went out to that class—someone should tell that instructor to stop overlapping her theories.

Interaction between teachers and students is always an important aspect of learning. One class offered their instructor this advice: "Try to be more calm when a question is asked. Don't look so surprised." Another class wanted their instructor to "stop interrupting the lecture to make sleeping accusations." Apparently, they wanted to be accused of sleeping at a time other than when they were doing it.

"Don't clip nails during presentations" was one of my favorite comments. I'm assuming the instructor was clipping his nails during student presentations and not during his own, but in either case, I agree that that could be distracting.

The following comments: "Jackie S. needs to be more careful with her knife and treat students with respect," and "Mike is good at his job and gives good suggestions, but should stop screaming and trying to scare people with knives in their hands," I'm hoping came from the Vet School.

From the School of Technology, where group work is emphasized, came this next suggestion. The students felt the next time the course was offered "there should be recourse for bad team members." They didn't mention how severe the recourse should be. Should it involve bodily harm? Pain? Maybe the group could punish their team member by making him take a class from the professor who clips his nails.

Sometimes a class would identify a problem without suggesting how to correct it. For example, "this course seems to be a low priority in the department. They stick us with whoever they can find," fits into this category. On the other hand, another class took responsibility for being part of the problem when they admitted at the end of the semester: "Instructors did the best they could with what they had to work with."

Well, I've digressed enough—it's time for me to get back to work.

Personally, I'm not going to worry about getting good evaluations from my students. I teach on the third floor.

In a building with no elevator.

A Day in the Life

When college professors have questions about teaching, they usually consult with their university's instructional development staff. That's where I come in. My name's Coffman. I'm an instructional developer.

8:02 a.m. Monday morning. I got my first call.

"I'd like to know what my students think of my class so far," Professor X said. "Could you come over and ask them?" It was halfway through the semester. A good time for him to find out.

"Hang on, professor. I'll be right there." I grabbed some evaluation sheets and dashed across campus.

I had no trouble finding the professor's classroom. It was right where he said it would be—in a Pharmacy lab in the basement of the pharmacy building. I stood in the back and surveyed the room.

A group of students was giving a presentation on various methods of contraception. One of the presenters pulled a paper bag off a cucumber mounted on a ring stand. This could get interesting. I pulled up a chair and got comfortable.

8:31 a.m. The group finished presenting. Then the professor

told the class he wanted feedback on how the course was going. He asked for their honest feedback, introduced me, and left the room.

That was my cue. I jumped to my feet. First, I explained that student evaluations were important because they helped instructors improve their classes. Then I asked the students to tell me what they liked about the course, and to give some suggestions on how they'd like to see the course changed for the second half of the semester. I was looking for the students' perceptions of the class. Nothing but their perceptions.

8:49 a.m. A young man wearing a baseball cap on backwards said his group didn't like the textbook. I broke out in a cold sweat. In this process, we don't accept complaints about a course. Only suggestions. I knew I'd better do something about it—fast. I took a deep breath.

"Could you rephrase that as a suggestion?" I asked.

The room got deathly quiet. All eyes turned to that student. Then he said: "We'd like to see this course get a book that has more charts and graphs and more current examples."

That was just one of their likes and suggestions, but yes! I'd done it again! I'd gone into a class and gotten constructive feedback so the instructor could improve his class!

9:01 a.m. I thanked the students and headed back to my office. I'd type up the results and meet with the professor the following day. I felt good. I was making a difference.

9:15 a.m. I stopped at the candy counter in the student union, bought a package of chewing gum, and was off to my next assignment. This one was going to be tougher. A department head had called me. One of his new faculty members was struggling with her class. He asked if I'd meet with her. I said that I would.

I arrived in Professor Neophyte's office at 9:29 a.m.

"What are your students upset about?" I asked, offering her a stick of gum. She declined the gum. I popped a piece in my mouth and sat back to listen.

"The course I'm teaching never used to have writing assignments. I've added some. The students don't want to do them. They also talk during my lectures."

"What year are they?" I probed.

"Seniors."

"How large is the class?"

"Eighty-five."

This one sure knew how to find trouble. If this was her first semester teaching, a class of 85 seniors was a rough way to begin.

I offered to sit in her lecture the next day to get a first-hand view of what was going on. As I left her office, I made a note to find a female faculty member for her to network with as soon as possible.

10:46 a.m. Back in my office. Professor "Came from Industry" was waiting to see me with some good news. This was an interesting case. This professor knew his stuff, but he'd been getting really poor course/instructor evaluations from his students. In fact, one student had written "Get this bozo out of the classroom" on an evaluation form. To improve his teaching, Professor "Industry" had taken some workshops that our Center on Teaching and Learning had offered, been videotaped so he could see himself teaching, and been mentored by an award-winning instructor on campus.

Students no longer thought of him as a "bozo." In fact, this morning he had a big grin on his face. He'd just been awarded tenure. Another instructional development success!

12:09 p.m. Had lunch at my desk. Tried not to drip my tuna salad sandwich onto the paper I was editing. Washed my milk down with two chocolate chip cookies.

1:03 p.m. Made some phone calls. Scheduled a time to observe Professor "Bo Vine's" large animal veterinary medicine class. After making the appointment, I sat back and tried to think what had happened the last time I visited this professor's class. Oh, yes. It came back to me. The last time I sat in his class, he reached into a cow's stomach through a hole in its side to demonstrate the kinds of things cows eat. I made a note to wear my boots that day. And to sit near the back of the room in case he started asking for volunteers.

2:15 p.m. Spent afternoon making phone calls. Needed to set up photo shoots for some workshops I was coordinating.

First, needed to get a picture of an absent-minded professor walking down the street who almost steps into freshly-poured cement. Had the professor. He was the featured speaker of a workshop on "The 10 biggest mistakes teachers make." Also needed to find some construction workers who would be pouring cement the following day. Not only got the construction workers and the cement, but also got a cement truck.

Next, needed a professor in a cap and gown posing with some five-year-olds. This professor was going to do a workshop on "Teaching the Students of 2020." Called the local pre-school. Got a teacher and a class.

For the third picture, I needed to call George, a master teacher on campus, and convince him to sit cross-legged on a hill dressed in a sheet (like a "guru"). George had taught Chemistry for over 35 years, had won a slew of teaching awards, and was going to share some of his techniques in a workshop. He agreed to wear the sheet, but declined sitting cross-legged on a hill. (He is a rather big fellow.) He said he'd do the picture if he could sit on a bench. Done.

4:59 p.m. I hung up the phone, took out a handkerchief, and wiped my brow. It'd been a full day. But that was my job. Trying to make instructors' jobs a little easier.

I turned out the lights and headed home.

It was time to watch Dragnet.

How Sex Changes as You Age

I went on a romantic weekend one time (when I was younger) and all I took was a red nightgown and a bottle of wine. Now that I'm older, making love is a lot more complicated. To begin with, I need a lot more equipment. For my most recent romantic weekend, I packed:

Rogaine (for my thinning hair)
My special shampoo and conditioner (for my thinning hair)
Retin-A (for my wrinkles)
Sunscreen (so I don't get any more wrinkles)
Eye drops (for my dry eyes)
Nose spray (for my dry nasal passages)
Dental floss and my special organic toothpaste
Chapstick (for my dry lips)
A special herbal ointment for the leg cramps I get after a day
of sightseeing
A pair of heavy wool socks (my feet are always cold)
My various assortment of herbs, vitamins, and prescriptions
A bottle of prune juice (to swallow my pills)

An exercise mat (for my back exercises)

My special down-filled pillow (so I could fall asleep)

Besides needing more equipment, then there's the timing. In my younger days, I'd throw a guy down on the ground and we'd make mad passionate love behind the nearest tree (or in the nearest cornfield). Priorities change as you get older. Now, before making love, I need to make sure the back door is locked, the cats are fed, and there's nothing I want to watch on TV.

The third way making love is more complicated has to do with timing. Sex is still spontaneous; you just have to plan the spontaneity. You check with each other. Are you both feeling well? Feeling up to it? Willing and able?

And, finally, of course, there's the positioning. Making love when you're older is like a sporting event. You want to have fun, but you also don't want to get hurt. For instance, here are some things you'll hear when Sam and I are in bed, getting ready to make love:

"Wait! Your hands are cold!"

"Wait! You're lying on my hair!"

"Wait—your beard is scratching me. Go shave."

"Hold on. I've got a leg cramp."

"Wait—I'm on the edge of the bed. Scoot over."

"Wait! My arm's getting crushed. Give me my arm back."

"Hold it—you're on my leg."

"Hang on—my nose is running. Could you hand me a tissue?"

"Wait a second—I have to sneeze."

"OW! That hurts my back."

"Stop. I can't breathe."

"Hold on for a sec. The weather's coming on."

Of course, after all that waiting—the timing's not right. We have to wait.

VACATION FUNNIES

The Grand Canyon

$\mathcal{D}$ear Steve, Arliss, Trena, Jenna, Colleen, Gary, Lyn, Lisette, Mark, Gary, Amie, Diane, Claire, and Feebee:

Whenever I get an email like this, the first thing I do is check to see where my name is on the list. If it's not first, my feelings are hurt. But then my super-ego explains to my ego that we can't always be first. What I'm saying is: if your name isn't first, don't take it personally. I love you all equally and the same. Next time you can be first.

As most of you know, Sam asked me what I wanted for my birthday and I told him I wanted to see the sunset over the Grand Canyon. So he took me. (Neat guy!) We flew out to Phoenix last Friday, then took a teeny plane to Flagstaff. On both flights, we would have opened the windows and stuck our heads out if we could. The landscape was amazing! Rocks. Brown rocks. Red rocks. Reddish-brown rocks. Sturdy, dark green evergreen trees. Rock formations going up. Rock formations going down. As far as you could see. It was nothing like the cornfields we have here in Indiana. I would have enjoyed it if we'd just spent our weekend flying over Arizona.

And the sun! So much sun! When I got off the plane, I pointed to the sky and asked the rental car person why everything was so bright. We don't have sun in Indiana. Do we?

We rented a car and drove to Williams, a darling little Western town. ("Darling" and "western" probably shouldn't be used in the same sentence.) We checked into the Grand Canyon Railway Hotel (tres elegant) noted for its lobby that has huge, colorful pictures of the Grand Canyon. Then we walked up and down the main street and bought postcards and refrigerator magnets in all the touristy gift shops. (Sam's really into refrigerator magnets.)

The next day we took the train from Williams to the Grand Canyon. Well, you know how crazy Sam is about trains . . . and about photography. He'd made reservations on the dome observation car, so we were able to see out the front windows, out the side windows, and overhead at the sky. More sunshine. More rocks. More scrubby evergreen trees. Sam took about 100 pictures just on the train trip. He shot a picture of the first car on the train, the second car (which looked exactly like the first car), the third car (ditto), the fourth car (you get the idea). He took a shot of the train turning right and a shot of the train turning left. He took a picture of the train climbing a hill and the train descending the hill. He took pictures of all the people who worked on the train, including the guitar player and the banjo player who entertained us. He took pictures of the trees, and pictures of the landscape that had no trees. I have no clue who's going to want to see all these pictures, but we have lots of them in case you ask.

Oh, speaking of pictures, Sam put on his professional photographer's hat and took pictures for everyone on vacation that weekend in Arizona . He'd see a husband taking a picture of his wife, and he'd go up and say "would you like me to take a picture of the two of you?" And they'd hand him their camera and show him how to use it, and he'd take their picture. Sometimes there was a whole line of people waiting to have their pictures taken. If I'd charged a nickel for all the pictures he took, we could have paid for our trip.

There's no way to describe the Grand Canyon. Let's start with its size. You know how you can run a mile (or walk a mile, or drive a mile)? Well, the Canyon is a mile deep. Then you look across to the other side. That's 10 miles across. Then you look to the left. The Canyon goes on for as far as you can see. And to the right. As far as you can see. It's all made out of rocks. We saw just a tiny part of the entire thing. When you look at a map, you can see it goes from the left hand side of Arizona all the way over to the right hand side.

I stood there in total awe. There's nothing like it in the world. I wanted to store the image in my brain so I could remember it, so I took a good look at it and had my eyes send the image to my brain. My brain had never seen anything like it, so it kicked the image back out. It thought it was a hallucination. I thought "That was weird" so I tried it again. I looked at the Canyon and sent the image to my brain, but there was nothing in my brain anything at all like it, so my brain kicked it back out again. You can't store a picture of the Grand Canyon in your memory. Nor can you take a picture of it. You can only stand, in awe, and look at it.

Which brings me to my fear of heights. The Grand Canyon is no place to go if you have a fear of heights. There's a paved walk along the rim of the canyon, but in most places there aren't any guard rails. We ran across a group of teenagers who were sitting at the top of a cliff (remember, it's a steep mile down) swinging their legs over the side. What were they thinking? Sam was almost that adventurous. He'd walk to the edge and peer over. I was a complete chicken. The only way I could look down to the bottom was to find a tree and wrap my arms around it. I was hugging a tree in all the pictures he took of me. (Note: there's an observation area that's completely enclosed with glass where you can stand and look if you're as scared of heights as I am.)

That night, on my birthday, we saw the sunset. There were some clouds in the sky, which was great, since the sun rays hit the clouds and streaked them with blue and pink. And the timing was perfect. Sunset came at 6:00 p.m., so I didn't even have to stay up for it.

But the most wonderful part of visiting the Grand Canyon is the food. In the newspaper with the shuttle bus information (they're trying to get cars out of the park, so they have this terrific, free, shuttle system), they had a section called "Day Hiking." One article was titled: "Double Your Calories, Double Your Fun." It reads: "Since you're at 7,000 feet, and you're going to be hiking, your best defense against illness and exhaustion is to eat a large breakfast, a full lunch, a snack every time you take a drink, and a rewarding full dinner at the end of the day. This is not a time to diet." Yes! Yes! Where else do you get permission to eat like that? I ate the whole time we were there. For one breakfast I had four large pancakes, a big bowl of scrambled eggs, four strips of bacon, and a huge bowl of oatmeal with brown sugar and fruit. I also drank a high calorie fruit smoothie. I didn't gain any weight! You've heard the term "heaven on earth"? If you want to go someplace and eat all you want without gaining weight, this is the place to go.

We stayed overnight, got up the next morning, and saw the

sunrise. Left that afternoon on the train back to Williams. If you go to the Grand Canyon, you must take the train ride. In the dome observation car. It's scenic and wonderfully entertaining. On the trip back to Williams, we looked out the window and saw two bandits on horses riding alongside the train. What did the engineer do but stop the train so the robber (singular) could board the train. (The second bandit was in charge of putting the horses back in the horse trailer.) By the time the robber came to our car, he was wiping his brow with his bandana and moving very slowly. He said he'd already robbed 10 cars on the train and that he was exhausted. To play along, people pulled out dollar bills and dropped them in his outstretched hat. It was really cute. Of course, it helped that we were all drinking complimentary champagne. That made it a lot more real! Ha!

Our trip home ended on an unexpected high. We boarded our plane again in Phoenix. You know how the pilot usually gets on the loudspeaker before you take off and introduces himself and his crew? Yesterday he didn't. I didn't think about it one way or the other. When we exited the plane, the pilot was standing there in his blue uniform saying goodbye to the passengers. I didn't notice him because I was thanking the flight attendant. Well, Sam always says "Good job, Sully" to the pilot when he gets off a plane. The pilots either roll their eyes or laugh good-naturedly. Well, this time when Sam said "Good job, Sully," the pilot grinned—just slightly. This time, it was "Sully" Sullenberger—the pilot who landed the plane on the Hudson River. As the passengers behind us deplaned, we heard them whispering excitedly to one another: "Did you see who that was?!"

It was so cool to have been so close to such a hero.

If you'd like to see a sunset over the Grand Canyon on your birthday, just ask Sam to take you. Between taking tourists' pictures and meeting the clerks in the gift shops, he made a lot of friends. I'm sure he'd be glad to go back to see them.

Anyway, that's my story. Email me when you can.

And put my name first.

Love,
Sally

How to Get on a Submarine

I thought there'd be a staircase.

When Sam's buddy Mitch, who recently retired from the Navy, invited Sam and me out to San Diego for a visit, he mentioned being able to get us a personal tour of a nuclear submarine. We were on the next plane. How many people get the chance to have a private tour of an active nuclear submarine?

I wasn't worried about the tour. I was a woman of the world. I'd been on the WWII German U-boat in Chicago's Museum of Science and Industry—twice. To get onboard, you just stepped through the door in the side of the ship.

I guess San Diego can have its share of bad weather which we got to experience when we arrived at the ship yard. It was blustery, windy, and cold—especially when we walked down the pier to the ship. Sam and I identified ourselves to the security guard on duty (who was expecting us), and he called the chief who was going to conduct our tour.

The chief began by walking Sam and me up and down the pier pointing out highlights about the ship. Then we stepped onto the ship and walked its length. Walking on top of a submarine. That was pretty cool. Then, he showed us the manhole we were going to climb into. I looked at it with awe and fascination, and then my brain told me there was no way I was going down that hole.

The thing is, we'd come all this way to see the sub. If I didn't go, I'd have to stand on the pier all morning. And it was cold on the pier. You know how I feel about being cold. I hate being cold as much as I hate climbing into dark, scary manholes. So I took a closer look. There was an inverted metal "U" handrail near the top of the manhole. The chief, who was young and athletic, grasped the "U" on the side closest to the manhole, and jumped down into it.

"You'll be fine, ma'am," he called. "Come on down."

I checked with my brain, and again, it said, "No way."

"Go ahead," Sam said encouragingly.

"You'll be fine, ma'am. Just step on the first step. You can do it. You'll be fine."

How did he know I'd be fine? He'd only just met me.

I squatted down and grasped the metal "U" bar. The problem was, I was on the wrong side of it. Remaining in my squatting position, I was going to have to change my direction 180 degrees, while at the same time lower my right foot down into the hole, hoping to find the first step, which I couldn't see. I took a deep breath and went ahead and did it before I could check in again with my brain. (Note to Navy: your top step needs to be closer to the top of the sub.)

Now that I'd made it to the top step, I realized I was going to have to unclasp the hands I was using to hold on for dear life and move them down, while at the same time moving my foot to the next step. Not an easy task when you're frozen in place. When I took my first step, someone yelled:

"Oh, my god!"

And I think it was me.

I took another step.

"Oh, my god!"

I took another step.

"Oh, my god!" I didn't know those words could be said in so many different ways.

"You're doing fine, ma'am. You're doing just fine."

I descended for a long time and was sort of getting the hang of it when the chief explained that with my *next* step, I was going to have to put the toes on my right foot on a *ledge* instead of on the ladder. That part of the ladder ended. Which meant that I was now going to have to totally let go of the ladder and reach below this (whatever it was) barrier before I could reconnect my hands to the ladder.

Need I remind you of my fear of heights and ladders?

We descended three levels (Sam says it was just two) with me screaming the whole way until we arrived at the bottom, into a group of grinning sailors.

I finally was able to relax. Then I realized: Hey. I was on the submarine! I'd made it! I was going to have a great story to tell my friends.

The sub was small, but the men on board seemed perfectly fine with it. There were about eight of us onboard, which seemed like plenty to me if you wanted your privacy, but they explained that the sub usually carries 150 men. They had to be kidding!

We stayed there for about two hours, talking and asking questions. The young men were proud of their ship and happy to show us around. They showed us the bridge, the steering wheel, the galley, the missile room, the dining room, the sleeping quarters, and the equipment that turned sea water into drinking water. And they let us look through the periscope at the skyline of San Diego and at the other ships in the shipyard.

I do have some suggestions for changing the interior of the sub, in case anyone from the Navy is reading this. First, the hallways should be widened. You have to suck your stomach in to pass someone going the other way. Second, I think you should finish off the ceilings. There were a lot of exposed wires. And third, you need to install at least one Lazy-Boy recliner. How do you expect people to relax at the end of the day if they can't stretch out in a recliner?

I probably could come up with other suggestions, but the chances of my ever climbing down that ladder again are nil.

Speaking of the ladder, when it was time to depart, I decided to be the first one off. Going up was going to be much easier than coming down. (Remember: I'm wearing my bulky winter coat and heavy boots.)

After about three steps, I realized that when going up, you don't have gravity working for you. And your feet don't have anything to do with getting yourself up. You have to use your arms to pull yourself up.

Now, I have zero upper body strength. There were three decks to climb (Sam insists it was only two), and no one to help me. My right leg started quivering. My left leg started quivering. My right arm started quivering. My left arm started quivering. Every part of me shook the whole long, miserable way up.

By some miracle, I managed to make it to the top. Where I was screwed. Remember how I said the top step on the ladder was really far from the top of the deck? So, when I got to the top step, I saw that I was going to have to move my hands from the ladder to that metal "U" bar which was WAY over my head, then somehow swing my fat, padded body up onto the deck with the hope of getting my right knee on the surface.

Had I waited and not been such a show-off (there's my ego again), I could have gone second on the ladder and had someone pull me out. But no, I had to go first. Given the energy I had left, I knew I had just one chance to accomplish this feat.

When Sam and the chief found me, they say I was flat on my stomach, clutching the deck and babbling to myself. They had to peel me off and carry me off the ship.

(Note to Navy: a staircase would make it a lot easier for everybody to get on and off your subs.)

By far the most memorable part of the tour was meeting and talking to the crew. They were sharp, professional, and patriotic. Sam and I left with a great sense of pride, realizing that we had men of that quality doing this work for us.

Since this is my book, I can write whatever I want, so I want to say "thank you" to all of our military personnel—from the potato peelers to the people on the front line. Because of you, I live in a safe country . . . and I can be a single woman who has the freedom to make my own decisions and live my own life.

Thank you for all that you do. And to all those who already "did."

Cruising on the High Seas

It was winter—again—in Indiana. I was having lunch with some friends who mentioned they were leaving soon to go see the Mayan ruins. How were they getting there, I asked. They were taking a cruise. I should come along.

I took a cruise once. It was designed for children. I was on a ship with 9,000 children who rode up and down the elevators, ran up and down the stairs, and ate fast food and ice cream for four days. I vowed never to take another cruise. But I needed a vacation. According to my travel agent, there was one room left on the ship. I booked it. I figured it would be just a hammock, on the lowest deck, next to the engine room. But I didn't care. Anything to get out of the snow.

The scariest part of the trip occurred when I was leaving. David, who drove me to the airport, wanted me to leave my winter coat in his car.

"I'm not leaving my coat!" I yelled, freaking out.

"You won't need it in Mexico," he coaxed, trying to peal it off me. "It's warm there."

"I'm not leaving my coat!" A tug of war ensued and we almost ripped the sleeves off. He won, and shooed me into the airport.

The cruise line had a shuttle from the New Orleans airport to the ship. Once aboard the ship, I quickly forgot my coat. The first thing I did was stretch out on a blue lounge chair on the upper deck. Indeed, there was sun! And it was warm. I examined my surroundings. Smiling waiters were bringing smiling people drinks. Smiling passengers looked happy that the smiling waiters were bringing them drinks. When I reached for my drink, I had to tilt my head to the side a bit, and water came out of my ear. Maybe that was why I'd had an earache all winter.

After getting some sun, I checked out my stateroom. The stateroom (I did have a bed, not a hammock), was small, but quite comfortable. The comedian on board said the staterooms were "Barbie" size and the TVs were "Ken size." That was about right. Although the room was small, the pampering I got from the room stewards was super-sized. The stewards came in two or three times a day (when I was gone) to replace my wet towels, make my bed, leave me brochures, and put clever little towel sculptures of different animals on my bed.

That evening I met my friends for dinner. The cruise was billed as "freestyle cruising" which meant you could dress any way you wanted (shorts, slacks, dressy dresses) and eat any time you wanted (basically, 24 hours a day). You simply found a dining room that matched how dressed up you wanted to be. The food was bountiful and sumptuous, and the service was to die for. All week I was called "Madam" (with the second syllable drawn out: "Ma-dahm."). I'm not "Ma-dahm" here at home. I'm either: "Hey." "Hey, you." or "Lady, what's your problem?" I quickly got used to the waiters putting my napkin in my lap for me and asking me how I was doing. In the mornings, when I ordered oatmeal, they'd hover over me with a bowl of brown sugar and ask me how much to pour on. At lunch, if I asked for catsup, they'd pour a small amount on a saucer-sized plate and put it next to my dinner plate. What a difference from serving myself catsup back home. Back home, I'd hold the bottle with one hand, slap it a million times with the other, then watch the catsup fly out across the table.

The next day was a full day "at sea," so I decided to check out the spa. How cool would that be, to be able to tell my friends back home that I had a spa treatment. For some insane reason, I decided to get acupuncture. It didn't dawn on me the implications of that decision until I was lying on the acupuncture table and realized it was rocking from side to side. Just how was the gal going to stab me with the needles if the two of us—and the table—were all moving? (She was great. She must have had a course in acupuncture school on how to sway with the boat.)

Actually, apart from sliding off the toilet the first time you go to the bathroom in the middle of the night (while you're still asleep), you quickly get used to the rocking.

The next day we docked at the first of our four ports. The ship travels at night which is really cool because by morning, you're at your new destination. How different from the camping trips my family used to take when I was growing up. I remember being stuffed into the backseat of the hot car along with my brother and sister, my dad not speaking because my mother hadn't read the map correctly and we ended up in the wrong state, and being told we should have gone to the bathroom at the last rest area and that we weren't going to stop again until dinnertime.

When there wasn't a dock to pull up to, the locals would bring their boats out to the ship to take us to shore. They wanted to be efficient (I think, to make money), so they juiced up the engines to the maximum and sped us to land. The small boat trips alone were worth going on the cruise for.

In Roatan, my friends and I played with the monkeys in Gumbalimba Park. They'd jump from the trees, swing onto your shoulders, and dig in your pockets to see if you had anything worth taking. To get to the monkeys, you had to cross a long suspension bridge high above the water. (Well, it was high to me.) Only eight people could be on the bridge at the same time. I ended up with the seven biggest people in our group. When they stepped on, the bridge started swinging. I started yelling advice like: "Slow down!" "Put your feet closer together!" "Stop rocking the bridge!"

Then I got a brainstorm. I decided to squat to lower my center of gravity and hold onto the middle ropes with my hands. Every few feet there was a vertical rope so I'd have to take my hands off the horizontal rope and move them forward. It took forever. Mine was probably the slowest crossing of anyone ever to cross that bridge. When I was almost across, my legs gave out and I had to stand up. I realized then that you can cross the bridge easily when you're standing because you can keep your hands on the top handrail without having to continually move them. Aargh!

There was entertainment every night onboard ship—a troupe of Second City actors, a magician (who was pretty good except for the time you could see him running offstage, when you weren't supposed to, because the fog machine didn't work right), a comedian, a ballerina from the Moscow ballet who danced on her toes (which was amazing since the ship that night was really rocking) and a talent show put on by the crew that rivaled the professional entertainment.

But the highlight of the trip was the Mayan ruins. They looked like pictures of the Egyptian pyramids. They were awesome. Standing there and looking up at them, you could feel the energy of the people that used to live there. One of the sites was at the top of a cliff overlooking the ocean. It was absolutely breath-taking. I sat on the rocks and meditated.

To my knowledge, the only embarrassing thing I did on the trip was my interaction with the shopping specialist on board ship. In my defense, I've never had my own shopping specialist. She was in charge of helping people buy diamonds when we got into the ports. Beautifully dressed, she'd stand by the grand piano in the lobby and hand out "discount coupons" for the diamond centers. Once, when I was exiting the ship, she asked if I'd like some coupons. I replied: "No, I'm just going to be looking for refrigerator magnets."

She looked appalled, then somehow managed to relax her face. I guess she didn't have many passengers who shopped solely for refrigerator magnets.

One of my girlfriends had been on 14 previous cruises. I could see why. It was like parting a thin curtain and stepping into another world. You don't know what's happening, either at home or in another part of the world. And you can't worry about anything. You stay completely in your pleasure-centered right brain. I found myself unable to even have a thought.

My brain at my job: Thought, thought, thought. Idea. Idea. Idea. Thought, thought, thought. Somewhat better idea. Thought,

thought, thought. Need to relax. Need to relax. Can't relax. Can't relax. Must think. Need to think. Have all these thoughts to think. Thought, thought, thought. Idea. Idea. Idea.

My brain on the cruise: Ahhh. I'm so relaxed. Yawn. Relaxed. So relaxed. Maybe I should try to have a thought. I haven't had one for awhile. Surely there's something I could have a thought about. Am trying. Am trying. Nope. No thoughts. Maybe I'll have one tomorrow. Relaxed, relaxed, relaxed.

When we disembarked, we had to go through customs. Although I like to joke with people, I'm dead serious when I'm standing in front of a customs officer, trying to get back into the country. Catherine and I went up to his desk together and handed him our passports, driver's licenses, and custom forms, where we had to declare what we were bringing back into the country. I had spent $38.00. On refrigerator magnets.

The customs officer asked me if I was bringing back any alcohol.

"No sir."

"Any food?"

"No sir."

"Did you visit any farms?"

"No, sir."

"Do you have any knives, weapons, or firearms?"

"No, sir."

Then he read my form.

"Are you bringing back vanilla?"

Then I remembered. I'd purchased six little bottles of vanilla.

"Yes, I am." Then it hit me. Maybe vanilla was considered to be food. So I began to babble: " Oh. Is vanilla FOOD? I didn't know it was food. They're gifts for my friends. I didn't know they were food. You see, I don't cook."

He looked at Catherine. "Do *you* cook?"

"No. I don't," she said honestly.

He stared at us and said, "Well, what do you people *do*?"

"We eat out," we both replied, hoping that wasn't going to stop us from being allowed back into the country.

He rolled his eyes and let us back in.

I'm already planning my next cruise. I'm thinking next year I could take a leave of absence from my job and be gone the whole winter.

I do know this. Riding the paddleboat at Indiana Beach this summer (a ride which is about 30 minutes long and goes about three miles per hour) is not going to have quite the same thrill.

CPSIA information can be obtained at www.ICGtesting.com
Printed in the USA
BVOW021718110911

270956BV00002B/12/P